MINISTRY TRAINING SCHOOL

LEVEL ONE

OUR NEW LIFE IN CHRIST

STUDENT EDITION

Ministry Training School, Level One: Our New Life In Christ (Student Edition)
Copyright © 2005 by Gospel Team Outreach, Inc.
ISBN: 1-932433-38-4
Requests for information should be addressed to:

Gospel Team Outreach
P.O. Box 25355
Fayetteville, NC 28314

All Scripture quotations, unless otherwise indicated, are taken from the *New King James Version* of the Bible.

Printed in the United States of America

DEDICATED TO THE BODY OF CHRIST

MAY THIS COURSE ENABLE YOU
TO GROW AND DEVELOP AS A CHRISTIAN

CONTENTS

CONGRATULATIONS, YOU ARE NOW A MEMBER OF GOD'S FAMILY! ENCOUNTERING Christ and the cross is a life-changing experience for each of us. To accept Jesus Christ as Savior and Lord is the most important decision a person can make. There is much to learn about this new life.

Each level of this course is designed to assist in our Christian growth and development. God has given us His Word, the Bible, as a manual by which to live. As we learn and apply truth to specific areas of our personal lives, we can experience greater levels of success and victory. It is God's will that we enjoy the blessings of a life well lived; however, we must understand that this requires change on our part.

This is a fast-paced curriculum that will launch us into an entirely different lifestyle, if we will follow the process. Take time to develop, ask questions, and allow the Lord to move in a great way. Simple assignments are placed at intervals throughout the Student's Edition for the purpose of getting better acquainted with the Word of God. Each will involve reading a passage of Scripture and filling in the blanks. The Teacher's Edition includes small group discussion topics and practical assignments, utilized at the discretion of the instructor. Teacher's Editions are available exclusively through *Gospel Team Outreach, Inc*. The address is located on the copyright page.

As we begin, it is important that we have a common starting point for all believers, regardless of maturity in Christ. The course will continue with greater depth of study as we progress. We thank you for making the commitment to Christ and to the diligent study of God's Word.

If you have not yet connected to a small group, you should seek to do so as soon as possible. Your group leader and pastoral team are committed to your success! It is vitally important to learn and grow in the grace of God in order to become all that the Lord wants us to be and experience all that He has planned for our lives.

Special thanks and appreciation go to all who had a hand in this extensive project. I want to especially recognize my wonderful wife, Vickie, for her patience and expertise in graphics and layout, and to Lisa, our secretary and editor. The elders of Cliffdale Christian Center are some of the best in God's kingdom. Thank you, men, for allowing me time to work on this endeavor. I pray we continue the journey together for God's glory.

In Christ,

Emory Goodman

OUR NEW LIFE IN CHRIST

"Therefore, if anyone is in Christ, he is a new creation; old things have passed away; behold, all things have become new."   *2 Corinthians 5:17*

There are several areas of our life that Christ desires to transform in order to assure our success and victory. When we are born into God's family, we are blessed with a new circle of friends with whom to socialize and build relationships. Experiencing change may seem difficult at times; however, old things will pass away and new things will come as we give ourselves to the Word of God. Through the course of time, we will see new friendships develop with people who are moving in the same direction we have chosen. We will no longer continue to be involved with improper sexual relationships, and we will recognize the Church as Christ's Body, desiring to find our place and do our part for God's glory. Three areas where change is most apparent involve our social life, sexual life, and church life. The following lessons will help us through this period of growth and transformation.

PART 1

OUR SOCIAL LIFE AND RELATIONSHIPS

Old Things Pass Away

How to be in Christ?

> ### Read The Following Passage And Fill In The Blanks
> #### 2 CORINTHIANS 5:17
>
> "Therefore, if anyone is in _____Christ_____, he is a new
>
> _____creation_____; old things have _____passed_____ away; behold,
>
> _____ALL_____ things have become new."

What Happens When We Receive Christ?

The truth is, we literally become a "new creation" in Christ the moment we are saved. Read the above Scripture again.

This means that God has a whole new life planned for us if we will commit to following Him.

This change will affect different areas of our life, not the least of which is our social life and relationships.

Dealing With Old And New Relationships

Many times, becoming a Christian involves having to make some very difficult decisions. This is particularly true in relationships with family and friends. It is true that Jesus comes to bring peace into our hearts and lives. However, it is also a fact of life that when we make a commitment to follow Christ, a measure of division or separation will result (Matthew 10:34-37). *Jesus did not come to bring peace but a sword...*

Jesus made very clear that those who follow Him have some responsibilities concerning this new life. There is more to being a Christian disciple than simply asking for forgiveness and waiting to go to heaven.

Read The Following Passage And Fill In The Blanks
MARK 8:34

"When He had called the people to Himself, with His disciples also, He said to them,

___Whoever___ desires to come after Me, let him

___deny___ himself, and take up his ___cross___,

and ___follow___ Me."

The Lord knows what is best for us. Following Christ ultimately leads to a better life. We can be assured that our Father has our best interests at heart. That is exactly why He sent Jesus to pay the penalty for our sins.

> *"Having been born again, not of corruptible seed but incorruptible, through the word of God which lives and abides forever."*   1 Peter 1:23

One result of the new birth is that we live differently than before. We are *in* the world, but not *of* the world.

There is a great conflict between light and darkness, good and evil. Believers are called out of sin and darkness and into the kingdom of light and love. As followers of Christ, we should not continue to walk in darkness. Obviously, this means we will have to learn how to manage relationships with others and not allow those who are worldly to have a negative effect on our lives. This involves looking for ways to have a positive impact on the lives of others, especially those who do not yet have Christ.

<u>Read The Following Passage And Fill In The Blanks</u>
1 Peter 2:9

"But you are a _____Chosen_____ generation, a _____royal_____

priesthood, a _____holy_____ nation, His own _____special_____

people, that you may proclaim the praises of Him who called you out of

_____darkness_____ into His marvelous _____light_____."

In Christ, we are God's own special people and are called to glorify the One who called us "out of darkness into His marvelous light" (1 Peter 2:9). We will accomplish this through our new lives.

Separate From The Past

"Therefore, "Come out from among them And be separate, says the Lord. Do not touch what is unclean, And I will receive you."   *2 Corinthians 6:17*

Separation may involve many areas of life and includes old friends and relationships, habits, and even thought patterns and behavior.

Develop New Friendships

Old friends will try to get us to fall back into old patterns. We must stand against the temptations of our past. Often, it is easier to roll back than to move forward, easier to fall down than to climb up. Many young Christians fall because they think they are strong enough to continue old relationships.

It is important that we seek to build new relationships, because it is difficult to stand without Christian friends around us. If we want friends, we must be friendly (Proverbs 18:24).

It helps to attend small groups where relationships are cultivated and understand that building friendships requires time and effort.

As young believers, it is important to walk with those who will help us grow strong.

If we walk away from associations that have a negative influence and seek those that have a positive impact, soon we will begin to influence others positively.

"He who walks with wise men will be wise, But the companion of fools will be destroyed."

Proverbs 13:20

Fellowship with believers is essential to good spiritual health.

"But if we walk in the light as He is in the light, we have fellowship with one another, and the blood of Jesus Christ His Son cleanses us from all sin."

1 John 1:7

Old Friends...New Friends

How do we handle old friends and relationships?

Often, it may be necessary to "cut off" some old relationships if:
- We are not able to socially interact with old friends without falling into the trap of sin.
- We have deep emotional or soul ties with individuals of the opposite sex.

We should not act self-righteous or "holier than thou"; however, we must seek to establish and maintain our Christian convictions. As believers, we should remain calm and at peace while speaking "the truth in love" to those who question or criticize us. People will be moved more by what they see than by what they hear. The best witness is the individual who "walks the walk" in peace, not striving with others. The person who has truly had an experience with Christ should never be at the mercy of those who simply know about Him. Believers need not be intimidated by questions or criticisms of those who have not yet received Christ.

 It is essential to remember that Christians never have the right to be rude! Most people will come to respect you as a life of integrity and truth is demonstrated; don't be overly concerned about those who are offended.

Read The Following Passage And Fill In The Blanks
1 PETER 3:15

"But _____ the Lord God in your _____,

and always be _____ to give a defense to everyone

who asks you a _____ for the hope that is in you, with

_____ and fear."

It is important to have a testimony to share when others inquire as to what has happened in our lives. Yes, we have changed. No, we are not the same as before; we no longer do the same things or talk the same way. We should be humble; we should not condemn others for their behavior when we know we used to be the same way. We must simply live out our new lives for others to see.

Revelation brings conviction; conviction builds character; character determines who we are in Christ.

Believers Need Not Be Ashamed

"For I am not ashamed of the gospel of Christ, for it is the power of God to salvation for everyone who believes, for the Jew first and also for the Greek."
Romans 1:16

You Are No Longer Seeking To Please Men, But God

"Or do I seek to please men? For if I still pleased men, I would not be a bondservant of Christ."
Galatians 1:10b

Be Strong In Your Confession; Remember The Words Of Christ

"But whoever denies Me before men, him I will also deny before My Father who is in heaven."
Matthew 10:33

Understand That You Are A "New Creation"; God's Light Has Shone In Your Heart

"For it is the God who commanded light to shine out of darkness, who has shone in our hearts to give the light of the knowledge of the glory of God in the face of Jesus Christ."
2 Corinthians 4:6

God Called You Out Of Darkness

"But you are a chosen generation, a royal priesthood, a holy nation, His own special people, that you may proclaim the praises of Him who called you out of darkness into His marvelous light."
1 Peter 2:9

You Were Darkness, But You Are Now Light

"For you were once darkness, but now you are light in the Lord. Walk as children of light."
Ephesians 5:8

Let Your Light Shine

"Let your light so shine before men, that they may see your good works and glorify your Father in heaven."
Matthew 5:16

Two things we can and should do are pray for lost friends and family members and be a positive Christian witness. Others may not understand the change that has occurred in us because they are still in darkness. Now our purpose is to seek to please God and walk in this new life. To be sure, it is a new and different lifestyle. Old things pass away, and everything becomes new!

This means that we have the opportunity to develop relationships with other believers and grow together. It is important for us to get connected with those who can help us in our walk with God. This is one reason that home groups are so essential. It is a fact that the small group offers the very best dynamic for growth as a Christian. We all need accountability and friendship.

The Lord is building His house, and He uses "living stones" in the construction of His temple.

Read The Following Passage And Fill In The Blanks
1 Peter 2:5

"You also, as living _____, are being built up a

spiritual _____, a holy _____,

to offer up spiritual _____acceptable to God

through Jesus Christ."

The Lord builds His dwelling place. He has chosen us to be His temple on the earth. Therefore, we must be separate from the world, even though we still live in the world. The truth is we do not think or live as we did before Christ became our Lord and Savior. Old things have passed away because we are moving in a new and different direction. Everything becomes new as we continue to grow and experience more of God.

We should not worry or fret about losing old friends who do not understand what has happened and simply love them and pray for them. We must keep our eyes upon the Lord and live according to His Word in order to enjoy the fullness of His favor and provision.

PART 2

OUR SEXUAL LIFE

God Made Sex To Be Enjoyed

Depending on age and experience, one of the areas of greatest struggle or victory in the believer's life is that of sexuality. This is an important part of life that simply cannot be ignored.

The truth is, God made sex good, and it is to be enjoyed by those who have entered into the covenant of marriage.

Read The Following Passage And Fill In The Blanks
HEBREWS 13:4

"Marriage is *honorable* among all, and the bed *undefiled*;

but _____ and _____ God will judge."

Many lose the blessing God intended because they do not wait. It is important to realize that God will bring the right person at the right time. We must first seek to honor the Lord in our lives. So often people are looking for love in all the wrong places and make serious mistakes that can affect the rest of their lives. No, God does not want us to be lonely and depressed. It is God's will that we live a life full of peace and joy. However, in order to experience the life that Christ came to give us, we must begin to give Him first place.

The First Relationship Between Man And Woman

God created man and said it was good. The Lord did not intend for man to be alone or unfruitful.

Read The Following Passage And Fill In The Blanks
GENESIS 2:18

"And the _____ God said, "It is not _____ that man should

be _____; I will make him a _____ comparable to him."

Because the Lord saw Adam's need, He created woman from the rib of man, and the two became one flesh (Genesis 2:21-24). To become "one flesh" refers to the consummation of the marriage covenant through sexual relationship.

The World's View

Many In Our Society Have The Idea That Sex Is Simply A Source Of Pleasure

The world has little or no understanding of the marriage covenant and has therefore perverted what God created and called good. Following are some important points to remember:
- Sexual appetite is natural. If left to itself, an appetite can easily develop into addiction. As a result, this addiction can lead to perversion.
- Sexual addiction is different from any other. Unlike addiction to tobacco, alcohol, or drugs, God gave us the desire for those of the opposite sex. He did not give us a natural desire for unnatural things.
- Sexual craving can lead to unnatural relations.

It is natural to have attraction between opposite genders. It is not natural to have sexual relations with those of the same gender.

"Likewise also the men, leaving the natural use of the woman, burned in their lust for one another, men with men committing what is shameful, and receiving in themselves the penalty of their error which was due." Romans 1:27

It is certainly not natural to have sexual relations with any other animal or beast.

"You shall not lie with a male as with a woman. It is an abomination. {23} 'Nor shall you mate with any animal, to defile yourself with it. Nor shall any woman stand before an animal to mate with it. It is perversion." Leviticus 18:22-23

Sex outside of marriage creates many difficulties:
  ◆ Unwanted marriage and/or pregnancy
  ◆ Abortion
  ◆ Sexually transmitted disease

The Biblical View

Sex Outside Of Marriage Is Sin

"But fornication and all uncleanness or covetousness, let it not even be named among you, as is fitting for saints."   *Ephesians 5:3*

"For this you know, that no fornicator, unclean person, nor covetous man, who is an idolater, has any inheritance in the kingdom of Christ and God."
                                    Ephesians 5:5

Fornication involves all sexual activity outside of the marriage relationship. This is not difficult to understand. Any form of harlotry, adultery, or incest is sin. Society will always try to push the issue or justify sinful behavior. Scripture is very clear on this matter. The Bible warns us to "flee" sexual sin. The word *flee* means "to run away or escape."

Read The Following Passage And Fill In The Blanks
1 CORINTHIANS 6:18-19

"Flee ___Sexual___ immorality. Every _____ that a man does is outside the body, but he who commits sexual _____ sins against his own _____. {19} Or do you not know that your body is the ___Temple___ of the Holy Spirit who is in you, whom you have from ___God___, and you are not your own?"

Apostle Paul lets us know, without a doubt, that our body belongs to the Lord, and we should seek to glorify Him with it. It does not glorify God if we live in bondage to sexual impurity. We should also realize the implications of our actions. When we engage in sexual relationships with someone, we are actually joining ourselves to them. This is more than mere sex. It is creating a tie because we yoke ourselves together. Believers are joined to the Lord and are one spirit with Him. Therefore, as Christians, we have no right to join ourselves to anyone whom we are not in covenant with.

"Do you not know that your bodies are members of Christ? Shall I then take the members of Christ and make them members of a harlot? Certainly not! {16} Or do you not know that he who is joined to a harlot is one body with her? For "the two," He says, "shall become one flesh." {17} But he who is joined to the Lord is one spirit with Him."
         1 Corinthians 6:15-17

Steps Involved In Sexual Sin

Sexual sin is not usually an immediate or spontaneous action. There are often steps that lead a person down a trail of sin. As we give place to thoughts that are not pure, a progression is set into motion. This trail leads us to sin if we do not take action to reverse the course. Many times this progression is as follows:

- We look.
- We lust.
- We linger.

In the book of James, we clearly see this process revealed.

Read The Following Passage And Fill In The Blanks
James 1:14-15   *progression*

"But each one is ___temptation___ when he is drawn away by his own ___desire___ and enticed. {15} Then, when desire has conceived, it gives birth to ___sin___; and sin, when it is full-grown, brings forth ___death___."

separated from God

King David's Example

David was one of the most successful men in the Bible. He went from being a relatively insignificant shepherd boy to becoming the king of Israel. In fact, many people would say that David was one of the greatest kings to ever live. God blessed this man and elevated him to a position of great prominence and wealth. Yet, the king was not without fault. In 2 Samuel chapters 11 and 12, we read a tale of sin and deception that was all the result of sexual appetite and desire left unchecked.

Note the following: *2 Samuel 11, 12*

- David should have been on the battlefield, not in the bedroom (11:1).
- He looked, and he lusted (11:2).
- He lingered (11:3).
- He sinned (11:4).
- David experienced consequences (11:5).
- He attempted to cover up sin by committing murder (11:15).
- The plot got deeper (11:26-27).

- David refused to repent on his own so God sent a prophet (12:1).
- David's anger was aroused (12:5).
- David was confronted with the truth; he was the sinner (12:7).
- David was reminded of God's calling and purpose (12:7-8).
- David's family suffered consequences (12:10).
- David repented (12:13).
- David was restored (12:24).

"He who covers his sins will not prosper, But whoever confesses and forsakes them will have mercy."
Proverbs 28:13

Establishing Guidelines To Protect From Sin

Keep this in mind: Any normal man who says he can never fall into sexual sin is boasting that he can claim the following:

- He loves God more than David.
- He is wiser than Solomon.
- He is stronger than Samson.

It is important to establish and maintain a strong spiritual perimeter. Following are some guidelines for keeping oneself free from sexual sin:

- Understand that sin brings serious consequences.
- Live to glorify Christ.
- Yield your bodily members to the Lord.
- Strengthen your relationship with Christ.
- Take ungodly thoughts captive.
- Develop the "mind of Christ" within you.
- Think on things that are good and pure.
- Put on the "whole armor of God."
- Don't live like the world lives.
- Don't be alone with others of the opposite gender!

Read The Following Passage And Fill In The Blanks
ROMANS 6:13-14

"And do not present your members as _____ of

unrighteousness to sin, but present yourselves to God as being _____

from the dead, and your members as instruments of *righteousness* _____

to God. {14} For sin shall not have *dominion* _____ over

you, for you are not under law but under grace."

OUR CHURCH LIFE

God's Family

When we were saved or "born-again," we became part of a great family, the family of God (Ephesians 3:15). God, through salvation, is not only our Creator, but also our Father. All those who know Him, through Christ, are our brothers and sisters. In fact, we are even related to each other by blood, the shed blood of Jesus.

Read The Following Passage And Fill In The Blanks
EPHESIANS 1:7

"In Him we have _____ through His blood, the

_____ of sins, according to the riches of His

_____."

The concept of the church being a family is seen throughout the New Testament. Family terminology is used to describe relationships:

- "Brother" (Acts 9:17)
- "Sister" (Romans 16:1)
- "Father" (1 Corinthians 4:15)
- "Mother" (Matthew 12:49-50)
- "The whole family" (Ephesians 3:15)

These biblical terms denote close relationships in the Body of Christ.

Healthy family and small group relationships provide protection, provision, accountability, mentoring, bonding, and nurturing. We need each other in order to grow up strong and healthy.

It is the will of the Father that His children love and accept one another and that we be united together to do His work. God has a beautiful work for His family to do here on the earth, and a certain structure to fit into while we are doing it. That structure is the spiritual "Body of Christ" called the "Church" (Ephesians 1:22-23; Romans 12:5).

God's Universal Church

It is God's intended purpose to have the Church strong and glorious in all of the earth. Christ, the Head, does not desire that we, the Body, be weak, powerless, or unproductive. In the last days, the Church is to shine like a bright light in a dark world.

"You are the light of the world. A city that is set on a hill cannot be hidden."
Matthew 5:14

We are living in what the Bible refers to as the "last days," and God's power, love, wisdom, and authority will be moving through the Church so much that it will cause nations to take notice of its Head, Jesus Christ. We are part of a nation within nations and a kingdom within kingdoms. Although the world may try to stop the Church, we will grow more powerful and more perfect until we become just like Christ.

Scripture reveals that the Church will be presented holy, glorious, and without spot or blemish (Ephesians 5:27). In fact, 1 John 4:17 says as Jesus is, "so are we in this world."

God's Local Church

As we begin to fit in and take our God-ordained place of service in the local assembly, the universal Church shall grow into the Lord's powerful vessel on the earth. All over the world, people are finding their place in the Body of Christ. New and powerful life is coming to the Church as God is pouring out His Spirit upon all flesh in a fresh, new way.

"And it shall come to pass afterward That I will pour out My Spirit on all flesh; Your sons and your daughters shall prophesy, Your old men shall dream dreams, Your young men shall see visions. {29} And also on My menservants and on My maidservants I will pour out My Spirit in those days."   *Joel 2:28-29*

Every follower of Christ has a place in His Body. Therefore, you have a special part to fill in the local church (1 Corinthians 12:12-27).

How We Can Find Our Special Place

"So we, being many, are one body in Christ, and individually members of one another."   *Romans 12:5*

There are some things we can do to find our place in the Body of Christ and be used for His glory. First of all, attend a local church that is preaching the Word and is open to the operation of the gifts of the Spirit. God will help us know which local church to become part of as we seek His will for our lives. Once the Lord has directed us to a local church, we should become a vital part of it and get active. We need to identify with that local assembly and be committed and loyal to the people. They are our immediate spiritual family, and we should meet with them on a regular, consistent basis.

Submit to the authority in the local church. The Lord has given each local church elders or leaders who feed and protect the people of God. They provide spiritual covering and direction and are there to help us grow in relationship with God and His people. Be open to learn and seek their help and counsel.

"And He Himself gave some to be apostles, some prophets, some evangelists, and some pastors and teachers, {12} for the equipping of the saints for the work of ministry, for the edifying of the body of Christ, {13} till we all come to the unity of the faith and of the knowledge of the Son of God, to a perfect man, to the measure of the stature of the fullness of Christ."   *Ephesians 4:11-13*

"Obey those who rule over you, and be submissive, for they watch out for your souls, as those who must give account. Let them do so with joy and not with grief, for that would be unprofitable for you."   *Hebrews 13:17*

Develop good friendships with people in the local church. We are all family, and we will be closer to some than to others. It is important to become involved in a small group in which we are comfortable. Be friendly and loving to all members of the local church. If a problem arises between a brother or a sister and ourselves, straighten it out immediately or seek spiritual counsel (Matthew 18:15-17).

Be open to fill areas of need in the church. God has a special function for everyone, and He is the One who has given us our abilities. Look for opportunities to serve. All of us should support the local church in the following:
  - Pray for each other and especially for leaders (1 Timothy 2:1, 2).
  - Become active and participate (1 Corinthians 14:26).
  - Give a tenth of the financial income (called the tithe), in addition to offerings for special needs (Malachi 3:10).

Listen to the messages preached from the pulpit, and apply them prayerfully. God will reveal His Word and His will through His ministers. Hear God's instruction no matter whom He chooses to speak through; it will bring life and health to you.

"My son, give attention to my words; Incline your ear to my sayings. {21} Do not let them depart from your eyes; Keep them in the midst of your heart; {22} For they are life to those who find them, And health to all their flesh."

Proverbs 4:20-22

Read The Following Passage And Fill In The Blanks
HEBREWS 10:24-25

"And let us _____ one another in order to stir up

_____ and good works, {25} not forsaking the assembling of ourselves

together, as is the manner of some, but _____ one

another, and so much the more as you see the Day approaching."

The New Testament Church Model

God is bringing His people into a measure of power and glory never before experienced. The keys for success that were in the early Church are available today. Those keys are recorded in Acts 2:42.

The Scripture reveals that we must continually devote ourselves to the following:
- The teaching of the apostles
- Fellowship with other Christians
- Breaking of bread in communion and fellowship
- Prayer with other Christians

Basic Needs Are Best Met In The Small Group/Family Setting

Listed below are the simple steps we should all take:
- Become part of a small group and get involved.
- Take responsibility for yourself and others.
- Pray for friends and family members outside of church.
- Invite everyone to become part of your small group.
- Continue Ministry Training School (MTS).

LESSON SUMMARY

BY NOW, IT SHOULD BE EVIDENT HOW AND WHY THE LORD DESIRES AND DIRECTS change in the life of the believer. We are called to be disciples of Christ and to follow Him as He leads and guides us through life. As we willfully obey His instructions, our lives are transformed. Our circle of friends begins to change, we desire to live a purer life free from sexual sin and bondage, and there is a strong sense of fitting into the Body of Christ. All of these things contribute to our success and overall victorious lifestyle as we are beginning to lay down our life, take up our cross, and follow Jesus Christ. We never have to fear where He is leading, because where we are going is better than where we used to be. We are a new creation in Christ, and indeed, old things have passed away. We do not need to spend too much time fretting over those old things. God is moving us into the Land of Promise. We must make the break with slavery in order to be truly free. Relationships will continue to change and develop as we commit ourselves to a life of faith and purity. Success, true success, will come as we learn to know and do the will of God. We simply must set our sights on what lies ahead, forgetting, or releasing, the things that are behind us. The future looks much better than the past!

"For He made Him who knew no sin to be sin for us, that we might become the righteousness of God in Him."   *2 Corinthians 5:21*

We are the righteousness of God in Christ. We are no longer slaves to sin, because it is no longer our nature to sin. It is the desire of our heart to please our Father in heaven, and He makes available all that we need to succeed. God will continue to direct our lives in all that we do and guide our steps along the way. The Lord wants to show us how to live lives that are holy, pure, acceptable, and just. No situation is too small for the Lord to direct, nor too difficult for Him to solve. All we must do is allow the Lord to give us new lives that are free, cleansed, and blessed!

QUESTIONS *for* REVIEW

1. What New Testament Scripture speaks of being a new creature in Christ and old things passing away?

   2 Cor 5:17

2. In what passage does Peter speak of being "called out of darkness"?

   1 Peter 2:9

3. Part one of this lesson lists four specific areas of life where believers must experience separation. List three.

   old friendships/relationships

   old behaviour/habits

   thought pattern

4. In what Scripture passage did God say, "It is not good that man should be alone"?

   Gen 2:18

5. Sexual appetite is natural.

   (True)   False

6. Sex outside of marriage is sin.

   (True)   False

7. Our body belongs to God, and we should seek to glorify Him with it.

     True   False

8. List the three steps that lead to sexual sin.

    look

    lust

    linger

9. It is important to establish a strong personal perimeter in order to stand against sexual sin.

     True   False

10. The Church is the Body of Christ.

    True   False

11. Jesus called believers "the light of the world."

    True   False

12. According to Acts 2:42, believers should commit to the following:

    a. Teaching of the apostles
    b. Fellowship with other Christians
    c. Prayer
    d. All of the above

NEW TESTAMENT BAPTISMS

"Then Peter said to them, "Repent, and let every one of you be baptized in the name of Jesus Christ for the remission of sins; and you shall receive the gift of the Holy Spirit."
Acts 2:38

The object of this lesson is to help the new believer understand the relevance of baptism from a biblical perspective. Baptism is not only an act of faith and obedience, it is also an act of identification with Christ. When a person receives Jesus and is saved, they are baptized into the Body of Christ and should follow Him in the obedience of water baptism as well as experience the infilling of God's Spirit. The Holy Spirit will give us comfort, protection, power to do His will, and help us pray more effectively. We will have victorious lives here on the earth and possess power to become overcomers of evil. In Scripture, there are seven types of baptism referred to. Three are most relevant to Christians today: baptism into Christ's Body, water baptism, and the Holy Spirit baptism. This lesson will give a basic view of these three and instruct us on how to apply each to our lives.

Baptism into:
> Christ's body
> water baptism
> Holy Spirit

PART 1

BAPTISM INTO CHRIST'S BODY

[handwritten: used 20 times in scripture]

[handwritten: Baptism : Greek baptisma — bapto]

[handwritten: Meaning to fully immerse, to dip under, to bury into]

Some Facts Related To Baptism

The word **baptism** is derived from the Greek word **baptisma** or more literally **bapto**. It is defined as follows: "to fully immerse, to dip under and up; to bury into regardless of the element used."

This word is used more than twenty times in Scripture. Seven different "baptisms" are referred to in the Bible. This lesson will focus on the three that are most relevant to the new believer:

♦ Baptism into Christ's Body (the Church) at conversion
♦ Water baptism, which establishes our being identified with the death, burial, and resurrection of the Lord
♦ Baptism in the Holy Spirit through which we are empowered for service

Baptized Into Christ And His Body

Basic Facts Regarding The Baptism "Into Christ"

When we received Christ as our Lord, we were actually placed into His Body, the Church. This work is carried out by the Holy Spirit and is a result of the miracle of conversion or "new birth."

The truth is, this is the only baptism that saves our soul and brings a person into the Body of Christ.

Our body an instrument of sin might be made inactive ineffective of sin/evil no longer slave of sin

---

Read The Following Passage And Fill In The Blanks
EPHESIANS 4:4-6

"There is one ___Body___ and one ___Spirit___, just as you were called in one hope of your calling; {5} one ___Lord___, one ___Faith___, one ___Baptism___; {6} one God and Father of all, who is above all, and through all, and in you all."

One baptism that saves for all eternity

According to Romans 6:3-7, believers are baptized into Christ and become identified with Him in the following:

- Death *(baptised into his death) [become one w/ Jesus by sharing His death]*
- Burial *through*
- Resurrection *– behave in newness of life [become one w/ Him by sharing resurrection]*

old self nailed to the cross with Jesus (unrenewed)

This is a miraculous work of the Holy Spirit in the Christian's life!

Purpose Of Baptism Into Christ

As we have already seen, believers are translated from the kingdom of darkness into the kingdom of light.

"He has delivered us from the power of darkness and conveyed us into the kingdom of the Son of His love, {14} in whom we have redemption through His blood, the forgiveness of sins."   *Colossians 1:13-14*

We see something powerful in the following:

- Believers are buried and raised with Christ.
  "Buried with Him in baptism, in which you also were raised with Him through faith in the working of God, who raised Him from the dead."
                    Colossians 2:12

- Believers are made one with Christ and seated with Him.
  "But God, who is rich in mercy, because of His great love with which He loved us, {5} even when we were dead in trespasses, made us alive together with Christ (by grace you have been saved), {6} and raised us up together, and made us sit together in the heavenly places in Christ Jesus."   *Ephesians 2:4-6*

- Believers must "put on Christ."

    "For as many of you as were baptized into Christ have put on Christ."

    Galatians 3:27

- We are to "put off the old man" and "put on the new man" which is renewed in knowledge.

    "Do not lie to one another, since you have put off the old man with his deeds, {10} and have put on the new man who is renewed in knowledge according to the image of Him who created him."

    Colossians 3:9-10

- Believers are placed into the Body of Christ as it pleases God.

    "But now God has set the members, each one of them, in the body just as He pleased."

    1 Corinthians 12:18

This Is All The Result Of Regeneration

"But when the kindness and the love of God our Savior toward man appeared, {5} not by works of righteousness which we have done, but according to His mercy He saved us, through the washing of regeneration and renewing of the Holy Spirit."

Titus 3:4-5

[handwritten: means again born]

The word *regeneration* means "(spiritual) rebirth, the state or the act of spiritual renovation; messianic restoration; regeneration." ***Spiritual renewal*** means "to renovate, make new, or restore to life."

[handwritten margin note: with man this isn't possible — with God all things are possible]

This clearly refers to the "again birth" by which believers are saved and set into the Body of Christ. In other words, believers in Christ are literally "born-again" at the time of conversion and become part of God's family.

Read The Following Passage And Fill In The Blanks
JOHN 3:3

"Jesus answered and said to him, "Most assuredly, I say to you, unless one is

___born___ ___again___, he cannot ___enter___

the kingdom of God."

---

fully immersed

WATER BAPTISM

Repent! Change heart + mind with change
not
repent to spray only with no
change

Basic Facts Regarding Water Baptism

In Scripture, water baptism is really a baptism unto repentance.

> *"I indeed baptize you with water unto repentance, but He who is coming after me is mightier than I, whose sandals I am not worthy to carry. He will baptize you with the Holy Spirit and fire."*   Matthew 3:11

Confession and forgiveness of sins is a prerequisite for this baptism. The reason is simple. If we have not confessed our sins and received forgiveness from God, we are not saved from the penalty of sin, which is death. No water has the power to save our souls. Only the blood of the Lamb, Jesus Christ, can cleanse us from sin.

> *"If we confess our sins, He is faithful and just to forgive us our sins and to cleanse us from all unrighteousness."*   1 John 1:9

Reasons To Be Water Baptized

The first reason to be baptized in water is that we should follow Christ's example.

In Matthew chapter 3, Jesus came to the Jordan River to be baptized by John the Baptist. At first, John questioned this behavior by the Lord. However, after Jesus explained the reason for His actions, John carried out the ordinance.

"But Jesus answered and said to him, "Permit it to be so now, for thus it is fitting for us to fulfill all righteousness." Then he allowed Him. {16} When He had been baptized, Jesus came up immediately from the water; and behold, the heavens were opened to Him, and He saw the Spirit of God descending like a dove and alighting upon Him."
Matthew 3:15-16

If Jesus needed to be baptized in order to fulfill "all righteousness," we should do the same.

The second reason is that baptism is a command found in the Word of God.

Read The Following Passage And Fill In The Blanks
MATTHEW 28:19

" _____Go_____ therefore and make _____disciples_____ of all the nations,
_____baptizing_____ them in the name of the Father and of the Son and of the Holy Spirit."

Water baptism does not remove sin or save us from its penalty, but it is very important and symbolic of the conversion process (death, burial, resurrection).

This is a "ceremonial" cleansing and outward display of what has already taken place on the inside of the believer. Only faith in the blood of Jesus Christ can make one righteous in the eyes of God.

"But if we walk in the light as He is in the light, we have fellowship with one another, and the blood of Jesus Christ His Son cleanses us from all sin."
1 John 1:7

Several New Testament Examples Of Water Baptism

Peter Preached Baptism To New Converts

"Then Peter said to them, "Repent, and let every one of you be baptized in the name of Jesus Christ for the remission of sins; and you shall receive the gift of the Holy Spirit. {39} "For the promise is to you and to your children, and to all who are afar off, as many as the Lord our God will call." {40} And with many other words he testified and exhorted them, saying, "Be saved from this perverse generation." {41} Then those who gladly received his word were baptized; and that day about three thousand souls were added to them."
Acts 2:38-41

"Can anyone forbid water, that these should not be baptized who have received the Holy Spirit just as we have?"
Acts 10:47

Philip Baptized Men, Women, And A Eunuch

"But when they believed Philip as he preached the things concerning the kingdom of God and the name of Jesus Christ, both men and women were baptized."
Acts 8:12

"Now as they went down the road, they came to some water. And the eunuch said, "See, here is water. What hinders me from being baptized?" {37} Then Philip said, "If you believe with all your heart, you may." And he answered and said, "I believe that Jesus Christ is the Son of God." {38} So he commanded the chariot to stand still. And both Philip and the eunuch went down into the water, and he baptized him."
Acts 8:36-38

Paul Had A Personal Experience

"Immediately there fell from his eyes something like scales, and he received his sight at once; and he arose and was baptized."
Acts 9:18

Lydia Was Saved And Baptized

"And when she and her household were baptized, she begged us, saying, "If you have judged me to be faithful to the Lord, come to my house and stay." So she persuaded us."
Acts 16:15

The Philippian Jailer Was Saved And Baptized

"And he brought them out and said, "Sirs, what must I do to be saved?" {31} So they said, "Believe on the Lord Jesus Christ, and you will be saved, you and your household." {32} Then they spoke the word of the Lord to him and to all who were in his house. {33} And he took them the same hour of the night and washed their stripes. And immediately he and all his family were baptized." Acts 16:30-33

Believers are to follow the example of Christ as an act of "sonship."

Read The Following Passage And Fill In The Blanks
MATTHEW 3:16-17

"When He had been ___baptized___, Jesus came up immediately from the ___water___; and behold, the heavens were opened to Him, and He saw the Spirit of God descending like a dove and alighting upon Him. {17} And suddenly a voice came from heaven, saying, "This is My beloved ___Son___, in whom I am well ___pleased___."

There appears to be some controversy over how to baptize in water. Is it to be carried out "in the name of Jesus," or "in the name of the Father, Son, and Holy Spirit"? Frankly, we see references of both in Scripture. The best advice might be to water baptize, "in the name of the Father, Son, Holy Spirit, and in the name of Jesus." Thus, we avoid vain debate and argument. To be sure, water baptism is fundamental to our Christian faith. It may or may not be an intensely spiritual experience for the individual; however, it is always an act of faith and obedience to Christ and His Word. There clearly seems to be no "set order" in which an individual must be baptized once he or she is baptized into Christ and His Body. Obviously, one must first be baptized into Christ in order for any other baptism experience to have true relevance. As to whether the individual must be immersed in water before being baptized in the Holy Spirit or with fire, etc., there is no set biblical pattern. For example, Cornelius was filled with the Spirit before being baptized in water (Acts 10).

The truth is that we should not be bound by a religious attitude or spirit when it comes to baptism. A person must first be born into the kingdom and family of God through the new birth. At that moment, they are saved and baptized into Christ. The order in which they are water baptized or receive the Holy Spirit is not the issue. The main thing is to experience both in whatever order they become available.

In addition, we should not get hung up on how the process of water baptism is carried out. Remember, God does not call us into religion; rather, He calls us into a relationship. How we follow the ordinances is open to interpretation. Jesus was baptized in a river. Does that mean we must all be baptized in the Jordan or any other river? Of course not!

The issue should not be whether or not we are baptized in the name of Jesus only or in the name of the Trinity (Father, Son, and Holy Spirit). The essential truth is that we are to follow Christ in the ordinance of baptism.

Act 1:4 Jesus Commanded them

PART 3

The house of Cornelius — No one touched him to received HS [handwritten]

HOLY SPIRIT

BAPTISM

John 14.16: And I will ask the Father + He will give you another Comforter the He may remain with you forever. [handwritten]

26: But the Comforter, the Holy Spirit, Whom the Father will Send in My name, He will teach you all things. And He will cause you to recall everything I have told you. [handwritten]

Basic Facts Regarding The Baptism In The Holy Spirit

Jesus is proclaimed as the One who baptizes in the Holy Spirit.

John the Baptist made the following statement:

> *"I indeed baptize you with water unto repentance, but He who is coming after me is mightier than I, whose sandals I am not worthy to carry. He will baptize you with the Holy Spirit and fire."*   Matthew 3:11

Jesus Himself Said That He Would Send The Spirit

> *"Nevertheless I tell you the truth. It is to your advantage that I go away; for if I do not go away, the Helper will not come to you; but if I depart, I will send Him to you."*   John 16:7

Pair-ra-clet [handwritten]

The "helper" or "comforter" is the Holy Spirit (John 14:16, 26; 15:26; 16:7).

Jesus asked the Father to send Holy Spirit [handwritten]

Prior to His departure from the earth, Jesus promised to send the Holy Spirit to comfort, teach, guide, and empower believers. The truth is, we need help in order to walk out this new life to which God has called us. None of us are capable in our own abilities of "doing greater works" (John 14:12) than Christ did. In fact, left to ourselves, we are doomed to failure. Every believer needs the help of the Holy Spirit in order to obey the Lord and fulfill His purposes.

This Experience Was Spoken Of Prophetically In The Old Testament

"And it shall come to pass afterward, that I will pour out my spirit upon all flesh; and your sons and your daughters shall prophesy, your old men shall dream dreams, your young men shall see visions: {29} And also upon the servants and upon the handmaids in those days will I pour out my spirit."

Joel 2:28-29, King James Version

Read The Following Passage And Fill In The Blanks
Ezekiel 36:26-27, King James Version

"A new _*heart*_ also will I give you, and a new _*Spirit*_ will I put within you: and I will take away the stony heart out of your flesh, and I will give you an _*heart*_ of flesh. {27} And I will put my _*Spirit*_ within you, and cause you to walk in my statutes, and ye shall keep my judgments, and do them."

Dynamis power

Old Testament prophets could only speak about the time when God would send His Spirit to fill the hearts and lives of His people. Before the Pentecost experience of Acts chapter 2, the Spirit could influence a person's life; however, the Spirit was not yet sent to fill hearts and lives.

This Baptism Is An Endowment Of Power For Service To God

"For John truly baptized with water, but you shall be baptized with the Holy Spirit not many days from now." {6} Therefore, when they had come together, they asked Him, saying, "Lord, will You at this time restore the kingdom to Israel?" {7} And He said to them, "It is not for you to know times or seasons which the Father has put in His own authority. {8} "But you shall receive power when the Holy Spirit has come upon you; and you shall be witnesses to Me in Jerusalem, and in all Judea and Samaria, and to the end of the earth."

Acts 1:5-8

It is important to note that in verse 4, Jesus commanded His disciples to wait for the promise of the Father to come. Again, this was a direct reference to the Holy

Spirit. The Father sent His Son to give us life. The Son sent the Spirit to give us power to overcome in this life. We may consider the following:

Jesus Sends The "Promise Of The Father"

"Behold, I send the Promise of My Father upon you; but tarry in the city of Jerusalem until you are endued with power from on high."   Luke 24:49

It Is For All Who Ask

"If you then, being evil, know how to give good gifts to your children, how much more will your heavenly Father give the Holy Spirit to those who ask Him!"   Luke 11:13

It Is For Those Who Obey

"And we are His witnesses to these things, and so also is the Holy Spirit whom God has given to those who obey Him."   Acts 5:32

Discord + deshar
nay
Lenders HS

Baptism Of Believers First Occurred On The Day Of Pentecost

Read The Following Passage And Fill In The Blanks
ACTS 2:1-4

"When the Day of Pentecost had fully come, they were all with ___one___

accord in one place. {2} And ___Suddenly___ there came a

sound from heaven, as of a rushing mighty wind, and it filled the whole house where

they were sitting. {3} Then there appeared to them divided tongues, as of

___fire___, and one sat upon each of them. {4} And they were all

___filled___ with the Holy Spirit and began to speak with other

___tongues (languages)___, as the Spirit gave them utterance."

There are several points to consider as we read about this event and experience. It is obvious that those gathered had experienced conviction that resulted in conversion. They were in "one accord," meaning they were in agreement and unity. It is also interesting that the Holy Spirit is depicted as "a rushing mighty wind," because many times throughout Scripture, the Spirit is seen as wind, breath, or air.

The passage says tongues as of "fire" sat on each of them. Of course, fire purifies and refines, a further step of preparation to receive God's indwelling Spirit. Finally, they were all filled and began to "speak with other tongues as the Spirit gave them utterance."

In addition, it is interesting how this points back to Mt. Sinai and Moses. Pentecost marks the giving of the Law of God to Moses on the fiftieth day after the deliverance of the Israelites from Egypt. The New Testament Day of Pentecost took place on the fiftieth day after Christ's resurrection. What the Law could not do, God sends His Spirit to do by filling the hearts and lives of those who believe.

Evidence Of Holy Spirit Baptism Was Spoken Of In The Gospel

Read The Following Passage And Fill In The Blanks
MARK 16:17

"And these _____Signs_____ will follow those who _____believe_____:

In My name they will cast out demons; they will speak with new tongues."

Evidence was experienced when the Spirit came.

Day Of Pentecost

"And they were all filled with the Holy Spirit and began to speak with other tongues, as the Spirit gave them utterance."   *Acts 2:4*

House Of Cornelius

"While Peter was still speaking these words, the Holy Spirit fell upon all those who heard the word. {45} And those of the circumcision who believed were astonished, as many as came with Peter, because the gift of the Holy Spirit had been poured out on the Gentiles also. {46} For they heard them speak with tongues and magnify God. Then Peter answered, {47} "Can anyone forbid water, that these should not be baptized who have received the Holy Spirit just as we have?"   *Acts 10:44-47*

Notice the progression in the Scripture above. The people first believed and were saved (baptized into Christ). Next, they experienced the infilling of the Holy Spirit with evidence of speaking with tongues. Afterward, they were baptized in water. This indicates that there is no set order of baptism experience so long as the individual first believes in Christ and is baptized into His Body at conversion.

Interestingly, this is again seen in the ministry of Apostle Paul.

Read the following Scripture passage.

"He said to them, "Did you receive the Holy Spirit when you believed?" So they said to him, "We have not so much as heard whether there is a Holy Spirit." {3} And he said to them, "Into what then were you baptized?" So they said, "Into John's baptism." {4} Then Paul said, "John indeed baptized with a baptism of repentance, saying to the people that they should believe on Him who would come after him, that is, on Christ Jesus." {5} When they heard this, they were baptized in the name of the Lord Jesus. {6} And when Paul had laid hands on them, the Holy Spirit came upon them, and they spoke with tongues and prophesied."   *Acts 19:2-6*

The people first believed and were baptized into Christ. Paul laid hands on them to receive the Holy Spirit, and they spoke with tongues. They had also previously been baptized unto repentance in water.

The Holy Spirit Helps Us Pray

"Likewise the Spirit also helps in our weaknesses. For we do not know what we should pray for as we ought, but the Spirit Himself makes intercession for us with groanings which cannot be uttered."   *Romans 8:26*

Let's face it. We do not always know how to pray in every situation. The fact is, we need the Spirit to help and direct our prayers. It is important to remember that to be "baptized" into Christ requires faith and obedience. Water baptism is similar in this regard. In the same manner, to receive the baptism in the Holy Spirit requires faith and obedience. God wants to give each of us a new language with which to glorify Him. The Holy Spirit is available to all who ask and have faith to receive. Speaking with tongues is simply an act of faith and obedience.

Jesus Said "Rivers Of Living Water" Would Flow

<u>Read The Following Passage And Fill In The Blanks</u>
JOHN 7:37-39

"On the last day, that great day of the feast, Jesus stood and cried out, saying, "If anyone

_thirst_____, let him come to Me and _drink_____.

{38} "He who _believes_____in Me, as the Scripture has said, out of

his _innermost being_____ will flow rivers of living water." {39} But this He

spoke concerning the _Spirit_____, whom those believing in Him

would _recieve_____; for the Holy Spirit was not yet

given, because Jesus was not yet glorified."

Again, we see a progression of steps. Jesus indicates that we must first thirst for the Spirit. Next, we must come and drink with faith in order to receive the Spirit and allow the "rivers of living water" to flow from our hearts. This is a great step of submission, faith, and obedience.

It is also interesting to note the time and place of this event. Jesus seemed to intentionally seize the opportunity when a great crowd was present for the conclusion of the feast. The preceding days involved sacrifice and offerings; however, events on this day probably included drawing water from the pool of Siloam.

On the last day of the feast, it was customary to perform a solemn ceremony in this manner: The priest filled a golden vial with water from the fountain of Siloam. This was typically mixed with wine and poured on the altar. Much fanfare would have been made, and it is viewed as probable that Jesus stood and cried while they were performing this ceremony.

The Lord was clearly stating that instead of depending on this ceremony of drawing water for ceremonial cleansing and refreshing, people could now come to Christ.

Jesus clearly makes reference to the Holy Spirit as being the source of life, light, love, and liberty, for the Spirit is the living water. It is also understood that influences of the Holy Spirit are often referred to metaphorically as water, fountains, wells, rivers, etc.

LESSON SUMMARY

WHEN WE ARE BORN AGAIN BY FAITH, WE ARE BAPTIZED INTO THE BODY OF Christ. In other words, the Lord places us into His Body as it pleases Him (1 Corinthians 12:18). We are individual members, each unique, yet now one with Christ. Following the example of Jesus, we identify with His death, burial, and resurrection through the act of water baptism. This is an outward demonstration of what has taken place within us. The old, corrupt man is dead and buried. The new man is raised in righteousness. Having become a part of Christ's Body, we are prepared to receive the Father's promise, His Spirit filling our life. The indwelling presence and fullness of the Holy Spirit can transform the most wretched life into one of tremendous success and righteousness as we learn to overcome sin and darkness. We receive new power and walk in a new realm of spiritual authority that brings glory and honor to our Lord. Time should be spent in fellowship with the Spirit of God every day. He will begin to lead, guide, and instruct us in the way that we should go. As we pray in the Spirit, we will be built up and strengthened.

"But you, beloved, building yourselves up on your most holy faith, praying in the Holy Spirit."
Jude 20

Our life is radically changed as we continue to walk by faith, identify with Christ, and be filled with His power. There is no greater blessing in life than to be redeemed from sin, placed into Christ's Body, and be filled with His wonderful Spirit. The joy of the Lord is our strength (Nehemiah 8:10), and no greater joy comes in this life than that of knowing the ransom for sin is paid, that we are in Christ and He is in us, and that we are filled with His Spirit. We are now cleansed and are a new creation. We must simply hold on to this truth and become a demonstration of it on the earth for the glory of God in heaven! This is the Father's will.

Preced
event - then - "suddenly"

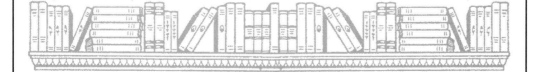

QUESTIONS *for* REVIEW

81.

1. How many types of baptisms are spoken of in Scripture?

    Seven

2. According to this lesson, what are the three most relevant baptisms in a believer's life?

Death	Chust body
burial	Water
ressurection	Holy Spirit

3. A person is baptized into Christ when he/she is saved.

    <u>True</u>   False

4. What is the Greek word for "baptism," and what is the definition?

    baptisma - bapto

    immerse fully in water

5. What are two reasons a believer should be water baptized?

    Confess faith publicly

    Commanded by God

    Follow Christ's example

6. What is the name of the river in which Jesus was baptized?

    Jordan

7. Water baptism saves us from sin.

    True   False

8. Prior to the Holy Spirit baptism, the believer must be water baptized.

    True   False

9. Believers first received the Holy Spirit with evidence of speaking with new tongues on the Day of Pentecost.

    (True)   False

10. The Holy Spirit helps believers pray.

    True   False

11. What was Jesus specifically referring to when He spoke of "rivers of living water"?

    Holy Spirit

STUDYING THE BIBLE

"Your word is a lamp to my feet and a light to my path."   *Psalm 119:105*

One of the first things a new believer in Christ needs to learn is how to effectively study the Bible. Many today profess to believe, but fall short in a methodical study of God's Word. A basic understanding of how we got our modern Bible should provide insight and provoke appreciation for God's Word. One of the objectives of this lesson is to help the student become a true disciple of Jesus Christ through developing a structured habit of studying the Word. We must get in the habit of using the Bible and become acquainted with its books. We need not be afraid to write notes in the margin of the Bible or use highlighting pens to mark verses that speak into our lives. The Bible is our guide; it will instruct, direct, shape, form, and mold our lives into what the Lord desires. We will become like Him as we learn more about Him. What follows is a fairly comprehensive study on how to accurately "divide the Word of truth."

PART 1

HISTORY
OF THE
ENGLISH BIBLE

The following section is intended to help the believer gain understanding and appreciation for the modern Bible. A tremendous price has been paid down through the ages as we see the Word of God pass from generation to generation. We must never take for granted the sacrifices made by those who have preceded us and made such a heritage available. The student will notice that the next several pages are written in a slightly different form. This is to allow for easier reading and comprehension.

The First Written Word

The story of how we got the English language Bible is, for the most part, the story of the Protestant Reformation, which began in the late fourteenth century with John Wycliffe. Indeed, if we go back more than just one thousand years, there is no language that resembles English as we know it today. The story of the Bible is much older than that, however.

The first recorded instance of God's Word actually being written was when the Lord Himself wrote it down in the form of ten commandments on the stone tablets delivered to Moses at the top of Mount Sinai. Biblical scholars believe this occurred between 1,400 BC and 1,500 BC. The language used was almost certainly an ancient form of Hebrew, the language of Old Covenant believers.

The earliest Scripture is generally considered to be the "Pentateuch," the first five books of the Bible: Genesis, Exodus, Leviticus, Numbers, and Deuteronomy…though there is some scholarly evidence to indicate that the Old

Testament book of Job may actually be the oldest book in the Bible. The Old Testament Scriptures were written in ancient Hebrew, a language substantially different than the Hebrew of today. These writings were passed down from generation to generation for thousands of years on scrolls made of animal skin.

Picture Languages

Hebrew has one thing in common with English: They are both "picture languages." Their words form a clear picture in your mind. As evidence of this, the first man to ever print the Scriptures in English, William Tyndale, once commented that Hebrew was ten times easier to translate into English than any other language. Tyndale would certainly be qualified to make such a statement, as he was so fluent in eight languages that it was said you would have thought any one of them to be his native tongue.

Old Testament Completed

By approximately 500 BC, the thirty-nine books that make up the Old Testament were completed and preserved in Hebrew on scrolls. As we approach the last few centuries before Christ, the Jewish historical books known as the Apocrypha were completed, yet they were recorded in Greek rather than Hebrew. By the end of the first century, the New Testament had been completed. It was preserved in Greek on papyrus, a thin paper-like material made from crushed and flattened stalks of a reed-like plant. The word *Bible* comes from the same Greek root word as *papyrus*. The papyrus sheets were bound, or tied together in a configuration much more similar to modern books than to an elongated scroll.

The Latin Vulgate

In 382 AD, an early church father, Jerome, translated the New Testament from its original Greek into Latin. This translation became known as the Latin Vulgate, (*Vulgate* meaning "vulgar or common"). He put a note next to the Apocrypha books stating that he did not know whether or not they were inspired Scripture, or just Jewish historical writings that accompanied the Old Testament.

The Apocrypha was kept as part of virtually every Bible scribed or printed from these early days until the mid-1880s, when it was removed from Protestant Bibles. Up until the 1880s, however, every Christian embraced the Apocrypha as part of the Bible, though debate continued as to whether or not the Apocrypha was inspired. There is no truth to the popular myth that there is something "Roman Catholic" about the Apocrypha, which stemmed from the fact that the Roman Catholics kept twelve of the fourteen Apocrypha books in their Bible, as the Protestants removed all of them. No real justification was ever given for the removal of these ancient Jewish writings from before the time of Christ, which had remained untouched and part of every Bible for nearly two thousand years.

By 500 AD, the Bible had been translated into over five hundred languages. Just one century later, by 600 AD, it had been restricted to only one language: the Latin Vulgate! The only organized and recognized church at that time in history was the Catholic Church of Rome, and they refused to allow the Scripture to be available in any language other than Latin. Those in possession of non-Latin Scriptures would be executed! This was because only the priests were educated to understand Latin, and this gave the church ultimate power. Nobody could question their "biblical" teachings, because few people other than priests could read Latin. The church capitalized on this forced-ignorance through the thousand-year period from 400 AD to 1,400 AD known as the "Dark and Middle Ages."

A Light In The Darkness

On the Scottish Island of Iona, in 563 AD, a man named *Columba* started a Bible college. For the next seven hundred years, this was the source of much of the non-Catholic, evangelical Bible teaching through the centuries of the Dark and Middle Ages. The students of this college were called *Culdees*, which means "certain stranger." The Culdees were a secret society. These men kept the remnant of the true Christian faith alive during the many centuries that led up to the Protestant Reformation.

The Protestant Reformation

John Wycliffe

In the late 1300s, the secret society of Culdees chose John Wycliffe to lead the world out of the Dark Ages. Wycliffe has been called the "Morning Star of the Reformation." The Protestant Reformation was about one thing: getting the Word of God back into the hands of the masses in their own native language, so that the corrupt church would be exposed and the message of salvation in Christ alone, by Scripture alone, through faith alone would be proclaimed again.

John Wycliffe, an Oxford professor, scholar, and theologian produced the first hand-written English language Bible manuscripts in the 1380s. Wycliffe was well-known throughout Europe for his opposition to the teaching of the organized church, which he believed to be contrary to the Bible. With the help of his followers, Wycliffe produced dozens of English language manuscript copies of the Scriptures. They were translated out of the Latin Vulgate, which was the only textual source available to Wycliffe. The Pope was so infuriated by his teachings and his translation of the Bible into English, that forty-four years after Wycliffe had died, he ordered the bones to be dug-up, crushed, and scattered in the river!

John Hus

One of Wycliffe's followers, John Hus, actively promoted Wycliffe's ideas. He also believed that people should be permitted to read the Bible in their own language, and they should oppose the tyranny of the Roman Church that threatened anyone possessing a non-Latin Bible with execution. Hus was burned at the stake in 1415, with Wycliffe's manuscript Bibles used as kindling for the fire. The last words of John Hus were, *"In one hundred years, God will raise up a man whose calls for reform cannot be suppressed."*

Martin Luther

Almost exactly one hundred years later, in 1517, Martin Luther nailed his famous "Ninety-five Theses of Contention" (a list of ninety-five issues of heretical theology and crimes of the Roman Catholic Church) onto the church door at Wittenberg. The prophecy of Hus had come true! Martin Luther went on to be the first man to print the Bible in the German language. *Foxe's Book of Martyrs* records that in that same year, 1517, seven people were burned at the stake by the Roman Catholic Church for the crime of teaching their children to say the "Lord's Prayer" in English rather than Latin.

Gutenberg Press

Johann Gutenberg invented the printing press in the 1450s, and the first publication produced was a Latin Bible. Ironically, though he had created what many believe to be the most important invention in history, Gutenberg was a victim of unscrupulous business associates who took control of his business and left him in poverty. Nevertheless, the invention of the movable-type printing press meant that Bibles and books could finally be effectively produced in large quantities in a short period of time. This was essential to the success of the Reformation.

In the 1490s, another Oxford professor by the name of Thomas Linacre decided to learn Greek. Linacre happened to be the personal physician to Henry VII and Henry VIII. After reading the Gospel accounts in Greek and comparing it to the Latin Vulgate, he wrote in his diary, "Either this (the original Greek) is not the Gospel...or we are not Christians." The Latin had become so corrupt that it no longer even preserved the message of the Gospel. However, the church still threatened to kill anyone who read the Scripture in any language other than Latin, even though Latin was not an original language of the Scriptures.

William Tyndale

William Tyndale was the captain and spiritual leader of the Army of Reformers. Tyndale holds the distinction of being the first man to ever print the New Testament in the English language. Tyndale was a true scholar and a genius, so fluent in eight languages that it was said one would think any one of them to be his native tongue. He is frequently referred to as the "Architect of the English Language" (even more so than William Shakespeare), as so many of the phrases Tyndale coined are still in our language today.

Martin Luther had a small head start on Tyndale, as Luther declared his intolerance for the Roman Church's corruption on Halloween in 1517 by nailing his "Ninety-five Theses" to the church door. Luther, who would be exiled in the months following the *Diet of Worms Council* in 1521 that was designed to martyr him, would translate the New Testament into German for the first time from the 1516 Greek-Latin New Testament of Erasmus and publish it in September of 1522. In the 1530s, he would go on to publish the entire Bible in German.

William Tyndale showed up on Luther's doorstep in Germany in 1525, and by year's end, had translated the New Testament into English. Tyndale had been forced to flee England because of the wide-spread rumor that his English New Testament project was underway, causing inquisitors and bounty hunters to be constantly on Tyndale's trail to arrest him and prevent his project. God foiled their plans, and in 1525-1526, the Tyndale New Testament became the first printed edition of Scripture in the English language.

They were burned as soon as the Bishop could confiscate them, but copies trickled through and actually ended up in the bedroom of Henry VIII. The more the King and Bishop resisted its distribution, the more fascinated the public at large became. The church declared it contained thousands of errors as they torched hundreds of New Testaments confiscated by the clergy, while in fact, they burned them because they could find no errors at all. One risked death by burning if caught in mere possession of Tyndale's forbidden books.

Having God's Word available to the public in the language of the common man, English, would have meant disaster to the church. No longer would they control

access to the Scriptures. If people were able to read the Bible in their own tongue, the church's income and power would crumble. They could not possibly continue to get away with selling indulgences (the forgiveness of sins) or selling the release of loved ones from a church-manufactured "purgatory." People would begin to challenge the church's authority if the church was exposed as a fraud and thief. The contradictions between what God's Word said and what the priests taught would open the public's eyes, and the truth would set them free from the grip of fear that the institutional church held. Salvation through faith, not works or donations, would be understood. The need for priests would vanish through the priesthood of all believers. The veneration of church-canonized Saints and Mary would be called into question. The availability of the Scriptures in English was the biggest threat, and neither side would give up without a fight.

Today, there are only two known copies left of Tyndale's 1525-26 First Edition. Any copies printed prior to 1570 are extremely valuable. Tyndale's flight was an inspiration to freedom-loving Englishmen who drew courage from the eleven years that he was hunted. Books and Bibles flowed into England in bales of cotton and sacks of flour. Ironically, Tyndale's biggest customer was the King's men, who would buy up every copy available to burn them…and Tyndale used their money to print even more! In the end, Tyndale was caught: betrayed by an Englishman whom he had befriended. Tyndale was incarcerated for five hundred days before he was strangled and burned at the stake in 1536. Tyndale's last words were, *"Oh Lord, open the King of England's eyes."* This prayer would be answered just three years later in 1539, when Henry VIII finally allowed, and even funded, the printing of an English Bible known as the "Great Bible."

Church Of England

It was not that Henry VIII had a change of conscience regarding publishing the Bible in English. His motives were more sinister, but the Lord sometimes uses the evil intentions of men to bring about His glory. Henry VIII had in fact, requested that the Pope permit him to divorce his wife and marry his mistress. The Pope refused. King Henry responded by marrying his mistress anyway (later having two of his many wives executed), and insulting the Pope by renouncing Roman Catholicism, taking England out from under Rome's religious control, and declaring himself as the reigning head of state to also be the new head of the church. This new branch of the Christian Church, neither Roman Catholic, nor truly Protestant, became known as the Anglican Church or the Church of England. King Henry acted essentially as its "Pope." His first act was to further defy the wishes of Rome by funding the printing of the Scriptures in English.

The ebb and flow of freedom continued through the 1540s and 1550s. After Henry VIII, Edward VI took the throne, and after his death, the reign of Queen "Bloody" Mary was the next obstacle to the printing of the Bible in English. She seemed possessed in her quest to return England to the Roman Church. In 1555, John "Thomas Matthew" Rogers and Thomas Cranmer were both burned at the stake. Mary went on to burn reformers at the stake by the hundreds for the "crime" of being a Protestant. This era was known as the Marian Exile, and the refugees fled from England with little hope of ever seeing their home or friends again.

The Geneva Bible

In the 1550s, the Church at Geneva, Switzerland, was very sympathetic to the reformer refugees and was one of only a few safe havens for a desperate people. Many of them met in Geneva, led by Myles Coverdale and John Foxe (publisher of the famous *Foxe's Book of Martyrs*, which is to this day the only exhaustive reference work on the persecution and martyrdom of early Christians and Protestants from the first century up to the mid-sixteenth century), as well as Thomas Sampson and William Whittingham. There, with the protection of the great theologian, John Calvin (author of the most famous theological book ever published, *Calvin's Institutes of the Christian Religion*), and John Knox, the great

Reformer of the Scottish Church, the Church of Geneva determined to produce a Bible that would educate their families while they continued in exile.

The New Testament was completed in 1557, and the complete Bible was first published in 1560. It became known as the Geneva Bible.

The Geneva Bible was the first Bible to add numbered verses to the chapters, so that referencing specific passages would be easier. Every chapter was also accompanied by extensive marginal notes and references so thorough and complete

that the Geneva Bible is also considered the first English "study" Bible. The Geneva Bible became the Bible of choice for over one hundred years of English speaking Christians. Between 1560 and 1644, at least 144 editions of this Bible were published. Examination of the 1611 King James Bible shows clearly that its translators were greatly influenced by the Geneva Bible. The Geneva Bible itself retains over 90% of William Tyndale's original English translation. The Geneva, in fact, remained more popular than the King James Version until decades after its original release in 1611! The Geneva holds the honor of being the first Bible taken to America, and the Bible of the Puritans and Pilgrims. It is truly the "Bible of the Protestant Reformation."

King James Bible

With the death of Elizabeth I, Prince James VI of Scotland became King James I of England. The Protestant clergy approached the new king in 1604 and announced their desire for a translation to replace the Bishop's Bible first printed in 1568. They knew that the Geneva Version had won the hearts of the people because of its excellent scholarship, accuracy, and exhaustive commentary. However, they did not want the controversial marginal notes (proclaiming the Pope an Anti-Christ, etc.). Essentially, the leaders of the church desired a Bible for the people, with scriptural references only for word clarification or cross-references.

This "translation to end all translations" (for a while at least) was the result of the combined effort of about fifty scholars. They took into consideration: The Tyndale New Testament, The Coverdale Bible, The Matthews Bible, The Great Bible, The Geneva Bible, and even The Rheims New Testament. The great revision of the Bishop's Bible had begun. From 1605 to 1606, the scholars engaged in private research. From 1607 to 1609, the work was assembled. In 1610, the work went to press, and in 1611, the first of the huge (sixteen inch tall) pulpit folios known today as the 1611 King James Bible came off the printing press.

These were produced so individuals could have their own personal copy of the Bible.

The Anglican Church's King James Bible took decades to overcome the more popular Protestant Church's Geneva Bible. One of the greatest ironies of history is that many Protestant Christian churches today embrace the King James Bible exclusively as the "only" legitimate English language translation, yet it is not even a Protestant translation! It was printed to compete with the Protestant Geneva Bible, by authorities, who throughout most of history were hostile to Protestants and killed them. While many Protestants are quick to assign the full blame of persecution to the Roman Catholic Church, it should be noted that even after England broke from Roman Catholicism in the 1500s, the Church of England (The Anglican Church) continued to persecute Protestants throughout the 1600s.

Throughout the 1600s, as the Puritans and the Pilgrims fled the religious persecution of England to cross the Atlantic and start a new, free nation in America, they took with them their precious Geneva Bible and rejected the king's Bible. America was founded upon the Geneva Bible, not the King James Bible.

Protestants today are largely unaware of their own history and of the Geneva Bible (which is textually 95% the same, but fifty years older than the King James Version, and not influenced by the Roman Catholic New Testament that the King James' translators admittedly took into consideration). Nevertheless, the King James Bible turned out to be an excellent and accurate translation, and it became the most printed book in the history of the world, and the only book with one billion copies in print. In fact, for over 250 years, until the appearance of the English Revised Version of 1881-1885, the King James Version reigned without much of a rival.

English Revised Version

It was not really until the 1880s that England's own planned replacement for their King James Bible, the English Revised Version (ERV) would become the first English language Bible to gain popular acceptance as a post-King James Version modern English Bible. The widespread popularity of this modern-English translation brought with it another curious characteristic: the absence of the fourteen apocryphal books.

Up until the 1880s, every Protestant Bible (not just Catholic Bibles) had eighty books, not sixty-six! Even the original 1611 King James contained the Apocrypha, and King James threatened anyone who dared to print the Bible without the Apocrypha with heavy fines and a year in jail. Only for the last 120 years has the Protestant Church rejected these books and removed them from their Bibles. This has left most modern-day Christians believing the popular myth that there is something "Roman Catholic" about the Apocrypha. There is, however, no truth in that myth. No widely accepted reason for the removal of the Apocrypha in the 1880s has ever been officially issued by a mainline Protestant denomination.

American Revised Version

The Americans responded to England's ERV Bible by publishing the nearly identical American Standard Version (ASV) in 1901. It was also widely accepted and

embraced by churches throughout America for many decades as the leading modern English version of the Bible. In 1971, it was again revised and called the New American Standard Version Bible (often referred to as the NASV, NASB, or NAS). This New American Standard Bible is considered by nearly all evangelical Christian scholars and translators today to be the most accurate, word-for-word translation of the original Greek and Hebrew Scriptures that has ever been produced in the modern English language. It remains the most popular version among theologians, professors, scholars, and seminary students today. Some, however, have taken issue with it because it is so direct and literal a translation (focused on accuracy), that it does not flow as easily in conversational English.

Modern Versions

Several modern versions of the Bible have become available in recent times. It is difficult to keep up with them all. Some are simply better reading editions, not necessarily popular because of accuracy. It is probably always best, when possible, to revert back to the original languages. This is the very reason that we will learn to use a Hebrew and Greek concordance. With this one reference book, students are given the ability to research any single word found in Scripture and accurately define its original meaning.

Stephen Covey, in his book *First Things First*, coined what has become a very popular phrase. He stated, "The main thing is to keep the main thing the main thing."

This is certainly true when considering the English Bible and how it has come into our hands today.

To say that only one English version is the inspired Word of God is presumptuous at best.

What does Scripture itself say?

> *"All Scripture is given by inspiration of God, and is profitable for doctrine, for reproof, for correction, for instruction in righteousness."*　　*2 Timothy 3:16*

Christians, and for that matter the world, would be better served if we remember to "keep the main thing the main thing."

It is essential that we continue to be diligent to study and show ourselves approved unto God (2 Timothy 2:15).

Symbols Of The Bible

There are many symbols for God's Word mentioned in the Bible.

- **Fire** - Burns, cleanses, and purges all that is contrary (Jeremiah 23:29)

- **Hammer** - Smashes, demolishes, builds up, strengthens (Jeremiah 23:29)

- **Lamp** - Instrument of light in dark places (Psalm 119:105)

- **Mirror** - Reveals what we are and can be in God (James 1:23)

- **Milk** - Nourishes the young in Christ (1 Peter 2:2)

- **Rod** - Measuring instrument and standard in all things (Ezekiel 40:7)

- **Seed** - Germinating, life-producing, full of God's life (1 Peter 1:23)

- **Sword** - Living, sharp, two-edged in its operation (Ephesians 6:17)

- **Water** - Life-giving, refreshing, cleansing (Ephesians 5:26)

- **Bread** - The bread of life, ever-fresh for daily use (John 6:35)

- **Anchor** - Holds the believer in safety through storms (Hebrews 6:18-19)

- **Honey** - Sweet to the taste (Psalm 19:10)

 An interesting note: If you count all the verses in the Bible and then divide by two, you would find the center verse of the Bible is Psalm 118:8. It is perhaps the best summary of the Word of God to man.

<u>Write Psalm 118:8</u>

_____

_____

_____

Conclusion

We must remember that the main purpose of the Protestant Reformation was to get the Bible out of the chains of being trapped in an ancient language that few could understand, and into the modern, spoken, conversational language of the present day. William Tyndale fought and died for the right to print the Bible in the common, spoken, modern English tongue of his day. He boldly told one official who criticized his efforts, *"If God spare my life, I will see to it that the boy who drives the plowshare knows more of the Scripture than you, Sir!"*

The Word of God is unchanging from generation to generation, but language is a dynamic and ever-changing form of communication. We, therefore, have a responsibility before God as Christians to make sure that each generation has a modern translation that they can easily understand, yet that does not sacrifice accuracy in any way. We should be ever mindful that believers are not called to worship the Bible, but rather the One who inspired it.

The believer in Christ must be committed to studying the Word of God. As the Holy Spirit guides and reveals truth, we develop into strong and fruitful disciples. This development requires the use of other reference books that will be discussed as well. There is not one English translation that is the only inspired version.

Much of the content of this section has been used with permission from "WWW.GREATSITE.COM" as the source.

PART 2

STUDYING GOD'S WORD

Psalm 19:7-9

Importance Of Studying The Word Of God

God's Word is a light that will direct our path to success in life as we study and apply the principles found within its pages. We should quickly establish a pattern of Bible reading and study.

It will be helpful to have the following available: a quiet place to read without interruption, a notebook, and a pen to write notes as the Spirit reveals truth.

Read The Following Passage And Fill In The Blanks
2 TIMOTHY 2:15

"Be _____ to present yourself _____

to God, a worker who does not need to be _____, rightly

dividing the _____ of truth."

It is important to study the Bible because of the following reasons:
- It is the Word of God to man (1 Thessalonians 2:13).
- It is alive and active (Hebrews 4:12).
- It effectually works in those who believe (1Thessalonians 2:13).
- It is good for doctrine, reproof, correction, and instruction (2 Timothy 3:16).

Concerning the Old Testament and New Testament, it is well said: The New is in the Old contained, and the Old is in the New explained. Each is complete, but one cannot be understood without the other. Scripture is its own interpreter.

How We Got The Bible

"He indeed was foreordained before the foundation of the world, but was manifest in these last times for you {21} who through Him believe in God, who raised Him from the dead and gave Him glory, so that your faith and hope are in God."
                                                                                            1 Peter 1:20-21

The Bible was given by inspiration of the Spirit of God. In other words, the Holy Spirit produced the Word through the writing hands of men. God brought infallible revelation through fallible men over a period of 1600 years. The Holy Spirit was the divine author; He spoke through approximately forty human writers.

Read The Following Passage And Fill In The Blanks
2 Timothy 3:16-17

"All _____Scripture_____ is given by _____

of God, and is profitable for _____, for

_____, for _____,

for _____ in righteousness, (17) that the man

of God may be _____, thoroughly

_____ for every good work."

Note the following biblical definitions:
+ **Inspiration** - Divinely breathed
+ **Doctrine** - Instruction (function or information), learning and teaching
+ **Reproof** - Conviction and admonishing
+ **Correction** - Straightening up again, rectification
+ **Instruction** - From "to train up a child," tutorage, education, chastisement, nurture

Saved by Grace through faith

If we, as believers in Christ, are going to "walk by faith," we must: *Hear* the Word, *believe* the Word, *confess* the Word, *do* the Word, and *stand* on the Word of God. That is why the Bible is fundamental to our success.

in Christ

Understanding The Doctrines Of The Bible

The Bible is not a book of do's and don'ts. However, it is a book of doctrines. The word *doctrine* means "teaching, instruction, or to teach the substance." All religions, true and false, are founded on various teachings and doctrines. When believed, received, and practiced, they determine the following:

◆ Character (what we are)
◆ Action (what we do)
◆ Destiny (where we go)

It has been accurately stated by Alexander Hamilton that "those who stand for nothing will fall for anything." This is the reason we must be established in the doctrines of God as found in the Scriptures (2 Timothy 3:14, 17).

Division Of Scriptures

You may have wondered why the Bible was written in two parts called the Old and New Testament. The reason is that God's revelation to man is progressive.

The Old Testament was actually preparatory to the New Testament and set forth the type and shadow of the Church.

> *"For whatever things were written before were written for our learning, that we through the patience and comfort of the Scriptures might have hope."*
> *Romans 15:4*

> *"Now all these things happened to them as examples, and they were written for our admonition, upon whom the ends of the ages have come."* *1 Corinthians 10:11*

There are thirty-nine books in the Old Testament. These include the History of Israel and the Law (seventeen books), Poetry (five books) and Prophecy (seventeen books).

There are a total of twenty-seven books in the New Testament. These include history in the form of the Gospel accounts and the Book of Acts as well as the Epistles and Prophecy.

Handwritten margin notes:
Hear
Believe
Confess
DO
Stand
teach substance of modesty + morality in life
Eph 4:14+15
".. no longer be children, tossed to + fro..."
Heb 6:1
"Truth is a pathway not a destination"

Press on

Express
Experiencial
Experience
Knowledge of God

- God's Word, being eternal, will never pass away (Isaiah 40:8).
- The Word of the Lord is forever settled in heaven (Psalm 119:89).
- Heaven and earth will pass away, but not the Word (Matthew 24:35).
- The worlds were framed by the Word of God (Hebrews 11:3).
- The Word is alive, powerful, sharp, and capable of accomplishing God's intended purpose (Hebrews 4:12; Isaiah 55:11).
- God spoke to Joshua and gave a promise for success and prosperity (Joshua 1:8).

Read The Following Passage And Fill In The Blanks
Joshua 1:8

"This _____ of the Law shall not depart from your _____,

but you shall _____ in it day and night, that you may observe to

_____ according to all that is written in it. For then you will make

your way _____, and then you will have good _____."

God's Word contains health and life for those who receive it (Proverbs 4:20-22).

The Word is essential because God's people are not to be tossed to and fro with every wind of doctrine (Ephesians 4:14). We need to be trained and have our minds renewed to understand and live according to God's truth. This will allow us to experience the measure of success and level of life the Lord has for those who love Him. The Bible states clearly that our carnal minds are contrary to God (Romans 8:7). If our minds are going to be "renewed," we must receive and act on the Word of God.

Apostle Paul admonishes believers to "cast down" imaginations and arguments that are contrary to the knowledge of God. He goes on to say that we must bring our thoughts into "captivity to the obedience of Christ," which can only be achieved as we learn to apply biblical principles to our lives.

The Model Bible Student

In the Old Testament, we read about a man named Ezra. He was a "scribe" or one of a "learned class" who studied and taught the Law of God and wrote ancient manuscripts. Ezra was also a model student.

Read The Following Passage And Fill In The Blanks
Ezra 7:10

"For Ezra had _____ his heart to _____

the Law of the LORD, and to _____ it, and to _____

statutes and ordinances in Israel."

Let's take a close look at this model student of the Word. (If we follow the example of Ezra, we also need to prepare, seek, do, and teach.)

Prepare means "to set, fix, order, establish, be stable, arrange priorities according to values, to take inventory."

We may ask ourselves, "Where is the Word in my life?" Time is often the number one enemy. The disciple of Christ must be determined and disciplined. This begins in the innermost part of the heart.

Seek means "to tread, or frequent to follow, search, to seek specifically to worship, to care for diligently."

This reveals our need for careful observation concerning the Word. Again, we must investigate and ask ourselves a question as we read the Bible. What does the passage say? We must read and meditate on the Word in order to receive insight and revelation. Don't be afraid to ask who, what, when, where, why, and how.

Do means "to do or make, commit, fashion, fulfill, maintain, observe and/or perform."

What principles are being illustrated? What changes must be made? This takes commitment to become a people who will do what God's Word instructs us to do (James 1:22).

Teach means "to instruct, to goad."

How do we share what we have learned? This requires outward communication and outward expression. At some point, we must talk the talk and walk the walk!

Proper Preparation For Receiving Understanding

The first prerequisite to good understanding is to be a child of God. It is not possible to receive clear understanding of God's Word if we are not saved by the blood of the Lamb, Jesus Christ (1 Corinthians 1:18). The Bible was written to teach God's people how to live and be successful. We also need the Holy Spirit to guide and teach us (John 14:26; 16:13). Unbelievers do not have the Spirit of God dwelling in them. That is one reason Paul encourages believers to be "filled with the Spirit" in Ephesians 5:18.

In order to get all that God has for us, it is imperative that we maintain a teachable attitude. This means we must approach the Word with a humble spirit and always seek to learn and grow. It is essential that we are spiritual and not carnal, because revelation is communicated by the Holy Spirit to our spirit and is revealed to our minds so that we can act on it.

> *"Now we have received, not the spirit of the world, but the Spirit who is from God, that we might know the things that have been freely given to us by God. {13} These things we also speak, not in words which man's wisdom teaches but which the Holy Spirit teaches, comparing spiritual things with spiritual. {14} But the natural man does not receive the things of the Spirit of God, for they are foolishness to him; nor can he know them, because they are spiritually discerned."*
> *1 Corinthians 2:12-14*

It is our personal responsibility to be diligent in the study of God's Word. If we will give ourselves to the Word and allow it to direct our paths, we will experience good success. We need to be diligent, study, receive the Word with humility, and begin to do what we have learned.

Methods Of Study

In order to "do" what the Word of God says, we must know and understand what it says!

> *"But be doers of the word, and not hearers only, deceiving yourselves."*
> *James 1:22*

One of the things that is clearly lacking in the Church today are suitable methods in regard to the study of God's Word. Many people seem to think it is adequate to simply pick up the Bible on occasion and read whatever happens to be on the page as the book opens. This is a lot like playing spiritual roulette.

 According to Webster's Dictionary, a method is "a suitable and convenient arrangement of things, proceedings or ideas; convenient order for transacting business, or for comprehending any complicated subject."

Simply stated, a **method** is a "convenient, suitably ordered procedure, and arrangement of biblical subjects." Most Christians lack an effective method for studying the Scriptures.

"And He opened their understanding, that they might comprehend the Scriptures."
Luke 24:45

The Holy Spirit will help us learn if we will apply ourselves to the Word of God and apply the Word to our lives. The sooner we break old patterns in our lifestyle and establish new ones, the quicker we will be on the path that leads to life. We can pray and ask the Lord to "open our understanding" so that we can better comprehend.

Basic Methods Of Study

Word Studies

Perhaps the most basic method of study is when we choose one word from Scripture and set out to discover all we can about it. By gaining comprehensive understanding of that one word, we will better understand the truth it represents and its context within a verse. Word studies are preparatory and foundational for what are called topical and passage studies. We will look at those in a moment.

Character Studies

This can be an inspiring method of study in which the lives of people in the Bible are examined. It is perhaps the least academic, but most life-oriented means of study. The main benefit is practical rather than doctrinal. The word *character* comes from the Greek word meaning "an impress, mark, or likeness." There are approximately 2,930 individuals referred to in Scripture. It is important not to confuse people with the same name. For example, there are thirty different Zachariahs and fifteen Jonathans in the Bible. Additionally, there are seven Marys and five different men called James. Also, it is necessary to identify the various names that may apply to the same individual: Peter, Simon, Simeon, and Cephas all refer to the same person.

A variety of questions could be posed in regard to the person being studied:
+ What does the name mean?
+ What is the ancestral background or heritage?
+ What were the political, religious, and cultural situations?
+ What great events took place in the lifetime?
+ Who were the friends or associates?
+ What character traits were exhibited?
+ What were some of the successes and failures?
+ What influence did he/she have on others?
+ What was the relationship with God like?
+ What lessons can be drawn from his/her life?
+ The list is almost endless!

Geographical Studies

This is one of the most foundational methods of biblical research. The aim of this type of study is to discover places of geographical and historical importance as well as possible prophetic and symbolic significance.

It is easiest if we list the name and meaning of the place. Be certain not to confuse places with the same name. Check the location on both old and modern biblical maps. Accumulate information from a Bible dictionary, encyclopedia, and other reference books as well.

Text Studies

Textual exposition can be approached in different ways depending on the student's desire. This type of study involves taking one or two verses that are complete in themselves. Then, break open the verse, make an outline, and use every component as the foundation on which to build a message. No doubt, this is a more difficult method. It requires greater thought, careful interpretation, and creativity in formulating an outline. It is important to see the progression in Bible study methods:
- A word study can lead to textual study.
- Textual study can easily progress on to a book study. This is due to the progressive nature of the Word; one thing just seems to lead to another if we keep looking.

Topical Studies

Topical studies arise from word studies. Topical study views an entire subject and often includes many Greek/Hebrew words. This type of study is a necessary step in the process of coming to a comprehensive knowledge of scriptural truth. Topical research takes a biblical subject and follows it through Scripture to all its related parts.

Studying favorite verses in the Bible may be beneficial, but the insights gained must be submitted to the whole of Scripture in regard to that subject in order to avoid error or teaching that is out of balance. To understand the biblical viewpoint of any subject, various Scriptures on that topic should be considered.

Passage Studies

Passage studies involve the selection of certain passages, chapters, or parts of a Bible book and extracting them as to theme and content, verse by verse. Passage study is expositional study and ultimately leads to book studies. Passage studies include word, textual, and sometimes place and character studies.

Book Studies

Probably the "ultimate" method of study, this is often a combination of word, character, geographical, textual, topical, and passage studies. A sound exposition of a book results from the combination and weaving together of all the above studies. Obviously, not every student of the Bible will be able or called to this form of study!

PART 3

THE STRONG'S CONCORDANCE

What Is A Concordance?

A concordance is an index of words that appears in the Bible and gives us each word's location in the Scripture. There is a reference book called the *Strong's Concordance* that gives a complete listing of all the words used in the King James Version of the Bible with references to all the places where the individual words occur in the Scriptures.

We might think that it is not necessary to learn how to use this reference book to be a Christian, and that may well be true. However, if we are going to be serious as disciples of Christ, it would certainly help to understand what the Bible is saying. When we read some passages in Scripture, we honestly may be reading an inaccurate translation. It pays to go back to the source, which is the original Greek or Hebrew. Fortunately, this does not require study of the different languages. All we need is the *Strong's Concordance*, because this is really a dictionary of biblical terms that refers to the original translation. Next to the Bible, a *Strong's Concordance* may prove to be the most valuable tool for study!

To Find A Particular Verse In The Bible

Be of good cheer! This book is not as difficult and intimidating as it first appears. Let's say we want to find a particular verse in the Bible. We know that it is "in there somewhere," but do not know or remember exactly where to find it. Simply pick up the *Strong's Concordance*. All we need to know is one word in the verse. Locate the word in the concordance. Having found the keyword in the concordance, read through the list of verses below it until the one we are looking for is recognized. That is really easy!

Definitions Of Hebrew And Greek Words

The Bible was written primarily in two languages: the Old Testament in Hebrew, or Chaldee, and the New Testament in Greek. The *Strong's Concordance* has a dictionary that contains each Hebrew and Greek word used in the Bible. This dictionary is divided into two distinct categories: Hebrew and Greek.

In a dictionary of the English language, each word is listed alphabetically. The information provided for each word gives the definition, but also mentions the language it is derived from, how it is pronounced, and even its synonyms and homonyms. In short, a dictionary gives more information than just definitions. The Hebrew and Greek dictionaries in your *Strong's Concordance* also provide more information than just the word's meaning.

When looking for verses, the more striking and significant the word recalled, the easier it will be to find the verse.

The dictionaries in the concordance list definitions much like a dictionary of the English language does. They are helpful if we want to know the meaning of a Hebrew or Greek word as it appears in the Bible.

Turn to the back of the *Strong's Concordance* and locate the Hebrew and Greek dictionaries. (The Hebrew dictionary is titled "Hebrew and Aramaic" dictionary. Older versions will say "Hebrew and Chaldee," pronounced "kal-dee").

We understand that most Bible students cannot read Hebrew and Greek; therefore, they do not know the alphabet of that language. Hence, they could not look up a word in these dictionaries. However, Dr. Strong provided a number for each Greek and Hebrew word that appears in the Bible so that we can look the words up numerically instead of alphabetically. Numbers for Hebrew words are upright, while numbers for Greek words are italicized.

Through the course of this study, we will learn how to use a *Strong's Concordance*. Sufficient time will be spent in a practical class workshop on proper use of this important tool. Please ask the teacher and/or small group leader for additional assistance if you need further clarification.

LESSON SUMMARY

A BASIC UNDERSTANDING OF HOW WE GOT OUR MODERN BIBLE SHOULD provide insight and provoke appreciation for God's Word. In order to be found faithful in the eyes of the Lord, we must be diligent to study and apply the Word to various areas of our lives. Just like Ezra, we should seek to become a model student that is capable of accurately dividing and sharing Scripture with others. Spending time in study, meditation, and application will bring us to a place of true discipleship. The Word must come to be our water, milk, bread, meat, and honey. It will provide a well-balanced and nutritious spiritual diet that will enable us to experience an overcoming lifestyle.

> *"I will delight myself in Your statutes; I will not forget Your word. {17} Deal bountifully with Your servant, That I may live and keep Your word."*
> *Psalm 119:16-17*

Every serious student of Scripture should become acquainted, not only with the Word as written in the Bible, but also with tools for study that help us become more knowledgeable and better equipped for service. The Holy Spirit will bring things to our remembrance (John 14:26), but we must first allow them to take root in our heart through regular study and meditation. If we have not already done so, we need to begin today to set aside time each day for Bible reading and reflection. We should apply a systematic process to our study and grow in knowledge and application of God's truth. Just as the Lord promised Joshua, He promises us today that we will have prosperity and good success through proper meditation and application of His Word.

> *"This Book of the Law shall not depart from your mouth, but you shall meditate in it day and night, that you may observe to do according to all that is written in it. For then you will make your way prosperous, and then you will have good success."*
> *Joshua 1:8*

God will write His laws and statutes on the tablets of our hearts as we apply ourselves to studying and practicing the Word (2 Corinthians 3:2-3). We simply must have a strong desire for, and take delight in, His holy Word.

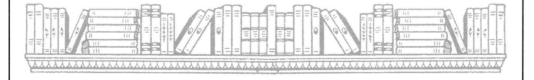

QUESTIONS *for* REVIEW

1. You should never write in your Bible.

    True   False

2. The Holy Spirit produced the Word through the writing hands of men.

    True   False

3. There were approximately seventy-nine to eighty-five human writers who wrote the Bible.

    True   False

4. The Bible is divided into two parts. What are they?

    _____

    _____

5. How many books are in the Old & New Testaments?

    a. Old - _____   b. New - _____

6. What is a word study?

    _____

    _____

    _____

    _____

7.   Which style is probably the least academic, but most life-oriented means of study?

   _____

8.   What is a concordance?

   _____

   _____

   _____

   _____

9.   The Bible was written in primarily two different languages. What are they?

   _____

10.   Write the books of the New Testament from memory.

   _____

   _____

   _____

   _____

   _____

   _____

   _____

KNOWING

JESUS

"For in Him dwells all the fullness of the Godhead bodily; {10} and you are complete in Him, who is the head of all principality and power."
Colossians 2:9-10

As we continue in our new life, it is vital for us to have a clear understanding of who Jesus is, what He has done on behalf of mankind, the power of His name, and the value of His blood. This understanding will result in a greater appreciation on the part of the believer, for in Christ, we find our identity. It is essential that we know what Christ has procured for us as an inheritance. In order to walk in victory, we must comprehend the principle of "justification by grace through faith." Today, that statement is considered to be a simple Protestant revelation, but it literally revolutionized the world during the period in history known as the Reformation. Many times, revelation leads to reformation, even in our individual lives. This lesson will reveal Jesus in a way that will be personal and intimate. The name of Jesus Christ is the most powerful name a Christian can speak.

PART 1

WHAT JESUS DID FOR US

[handwritten annotation: 2 Cor 4:4 In whom the god of this world hath blinded the minds of them which believe not, lest the light of the glorious gospel of Christ, who is the image of God, should shine unto them]

Jesus, The Eternal Son Of God

The first essential truth that we must grasp is that Jesus Christ is the eternal Son of God. He was the "express image" (2 Corinthians 4:4) of God in bodily form on the earth. Having accomplished the purpose for which He left glory, He returned and sat at the "right hand of Majesty on high" (Hebrews 1:3).

Read Hebrews 1:1-6. Jesus Christ did not become God as some religions teach. He was God in the beginning, and when this world as we know it has passed away, He will still be God.

"Jesus Christ is the same yesterday, today, and forever."　　　*Hebrews 13:8*

When man was originally made in the garden, the Godhead spoke in agreement saying, "Let Us make man in Our image, according to Our likeness" (Genesis 1:26). This points to the plurality commonly referred to as the Trinity: One God in three distinct personalities (Father, Son, and Holy Spirit).

Jesus, the Son of God, was the Word made flesh. He came to the earth for one reason: to fulfill the will of the Father who sent Him.

"For I have come down from heaven, not to do My own will, but the will of Him who sent Me."　　　*John 6:38*

"And the Word became flesh and dwelt among us, and we beheld His glory, the glory as of the only begotten of the Father, full of grace and truth."　*John 1:14*

The plan of God could only be carried out through His eternal Son taking on the flesh of man and shedding His perfect and sinless blood. This means that Christ was God in the flesh. As such, He laid His own will aside and suffered in order to fulfill the will of the One who sent Him. Being man, Jesus agonized over the cup of death, knowing what was involved (Luke 22:42-44).

The Son of God laid down His life willingly. No man could take it from Him.

> *"Therefore My Father loves Me, because I lay down My life that I may take it again. {18} "No one takes it from Me, but I lay it down of Myself. I have power to lay it down, and I have power to take it again. This command I have received from My Father."*
> *John 10:17-18*

It is truly difficult to comprehend, but Jesus' suffering and death pleased the Father. How could this be? It was due to the fact that through His death, burial, and resurrection, sinful man could once again be reconciled to a holy God. Man and his Creator could walk in fellowship as in the beginning.

Read The Following Passage And Fill In The Blanks
COLOSSIANS 1:21-22

"And you, who once were _alienated_ and enemies in your mind by

wicked works, yet now He has _reconciled_

{22} in the body of His flesh through _death_, to present

you holy, and _unblameable_, and above reproach in His sight."

Jesus Christ made peace with God, through the blood of the cross, on behalf of alienated man. This pleased the Father. No longer would the blood of animals be shed for a sacrifice that was still not capable of fully restoring man into right standing in the eyes of God. The full redemptive price was now paid through the perfect blood of a man who was tempted in every way such is common to us today, yet had no sin (Hebrews 4:15).

Old Testament Prophecies Fulfilled

- not to destroy the Law but to fulfill

Christ did not come to do away with the Law; rather, He came to fulfill it (Matthew 5:17). The birth, life, death, resurrection, and ascension of Christ are all events that had been spoken of hundreds of years before they occurred on the earth. God spoke through His prophets in order to prepare the people.

[handwritten note at top: unto us a Child is born a Son is given]

Isaiah, the prophet, spoke very clearly in regard to the coming Savior and what would be accomplished through His sacrifices. Not only did Isaiah speak of the birth of Christ in passages such as Isaiah 9:6, he also spoke in detail concerning the death of our Lord (Isaiah 53:9-12). *[handwritten: made grave w/ wicked... no deceit in his mouth]*

While suffering on the cross, the Son of God carried our sins, sorrows, sicknesses, and the full punishment for our iniquities.

Read The Following Passage And Fill In The Blanks
ISAIAH 53:4-6

"Surely He has borne our __*grief*__ And carried our __*sorrow*__; Yet we esteemed Him stricken, Smitten by God, and afflicted. {5} But He was __*wounded*__ for our transgressions, He was __*bruised*__ for our iniquities; The chastisement for our __*peace*__ was upon Him, And by His stripes we are __*healed*__. {6} All we like sheep have gone __*astray*__; We have turned, every one, to his own way; And the LORD has laid on Him the __*iniquity*__ of us all."

Jesus literally took our grief and sorrow. The penalty for our sin was laid on Him. In fact, He became sin for us at Calvary (2 Corinthians 5:21). Many believers do not realize that Jesus took the curse of sin and sickness upon His own body. Therefore, "by His stripes we are healed" (Isaiah 53:5; 1 Peter 2:24). The torture and crucifixion were so gruesome that even the physical appearance of Jesus was changed (Isaiah 52:14).

The book of Psalms has several prophetic passages concerning the coming Messiah.

A close look at chapters such as Psalm 22 (His death on the cross), Psalm 88 (His experience in the pit), and Psalm 18 (His deliverance from hell) are written not only in regard to the personal experience of the writer. These are also prophetic Scriptures that point to the Redeemer. Jesus Himself spoke of His coming experience.

"For as Jonah was three days and three nights in the belly of the great fish, so will the Son of Man be three days and three nights in the heart of the earth."
Matthew 12:40

"It Is Finished"

"So when Jesus had received the sour wine, He said, "It is finished!" And bowing His head, He gave up His spirit."   *John 19:30*

Let's examine some of what was accomplished when Christ proclaimed, "It is finished!"

First of all, we must understand that the Son of God was lifted up as judgment against sin. In other words, sin would no longer have power to dictate and control God's people. Man could finally be freed from sin's bondage because the old covenant was now fulfilled, and the new covenant was established through Christ's blood. The veil that separated man and God was removed. This gives us open access to our Creator. In fact, God calls us into fellowship with Him. We must, however, come by way of Jesus Christ's blood.

In the Old Testament tabernacle, there was a curtain, or veil, that divided the two interior rooms. One area was called the Holy Place; the other was the Most Holy or Holy of Holies.

This second chamber contained the Ark of the Tabernacle. This was where the presence and glory of God dwelt.

Although anyone could come to the outer court and offer sacrifices to God, only the priests could actually minister in the Holy Place. The Holy of Holies could only be entered once a year by the high priest. He would come to offer a sacrifice to God for the sins of the people. This happened on what was called the Day of Atonement. When Jesus died on the cross, something very significant took place.

Read The Following Passage And Fill In The Blanks
MATTHEW 27:50-51

"And _____ cried out again with a loud voice, and yielded up His

spirit. {51} Then, behold, the _____ of the temple was torn in

_____ from top to bottom; and the _____ quaked,

and the _____ were split,"

The veil was torn in two from top to bottom. This opened the door of entrance for man to come to God. Of course, this was also the fulfillment of all Scriptures written in regard to the suffering of the Messiah.

Of special note is the fact that Satan was defeated once and for all. It is true that our adversary is still alive and well and operating throughout the earth today. However, Christ stripped the enemy of the authority granted him through the sin of Adam. Remember, that in the beginning, God gave mankind full authority to exercise dominion over the earth. Through willing disobedience, man relinquished this authority to Satan. Jesus Christ triumphed over hell, death, and the grave, and in so doing, He has won the victory for those who believe in Him. Thus, the reign of terror, death, and sin has ended. Salvation and redemption have been made available to whosoever believes and accepts Christ as the sacrifice for their sin. The death penalty has been lifted. The enemy has no legal hold on God's people because of Christ's love and obedience. To be *justified* means "believers have been declared 'not guilty' by the eternal Judge of the universe."

"Much more then, having now been justified by His blood, we shall be saved from wrath through Him."   Romans 5:9

In addition, the atonement for sin brought healing from sickness and disease. This is what the Scripture means when it declares "by His stripes we are healed." As surely as Christ, the Lamb of God, took upon Himself our sin, He bore our sickness and disease. The Word of God makes clear that a price has been paid for our sin and our sickness. We have the legal right to be saved, healed, and delivered because Jesus Christ paid the price in full for our freedom. Now we can receive a new heart and the fullness of God's Spirit and power.

All of this was spoken of by holy men of God in the Old Testament.

Read The Following Passage And Fill In The Blanks
EZEKIEL 36:26-27

"I will give you a new _____ and put a new

_____ within you; I will take the heart of _____

out of your flesh and give you a heart of _____. {27}

"I will put _____ Spirit within you and cause you to

walk in _____ statutes, and you will keep

_____ judgments and do them."

God's people now have freedom to believe and obey the Lord. This results in lives that are truly blessed with success and prosperity.

Jesus Sat Down At God's Right Hand

"Which He worked in Christ when He raised Him from the dead and seated Him at His right hand in the heavenly places."   *Ephesians 1:20*

Let's look at some of the most significant things God accomplished through His eternal Son according to Ephesians 1:20-22:

- Raised Jesus from the dead (Ephesians 1:20)
- Exalted Jesus at His own right hand (Ephesians 1:20)
- Gave Jesus power over ALL powers (Ephesians 1:21)
- Gave Jesus a name above every name (Ephesians 1:21)
- Put all things under Jesus' feet (Ephesians 1:22)
- Gave Jesus headship of the Church (Ephesians 1:22)

Having fulfilled His purpose on the earth, Jesus was delivered up to His rightful position in glory.

Romans 4:25 says that Jesus was "delivered up because of our offenses," and He was "raised because of our justification." As a result, we are declared free from sin and guilt. Believers are made righteous by faith and can receive peace and reconciliation with God. Another great blessing is that we receive God's divine nature. In other words, it is no longer our nature to sin and rebel against God. Read 2 Peter 1:2-4.

All of this actually signaled the beginning of the end for God's adversary, Satan. It is no wonder that the enemy is so opposed to believers and the Church today. When you think about it, this was the very reason for which Christ came: to defeat the powers of darkness that had wielded authority over the earth and its inhabitants.

1 John 3:8 makes this very clear as it states, "For this purpose the Son of God was manifested, that He might destroy the works of the devil."

The enemy uses fear, terror, and manipulation to keep mankind in slavery and bondage. Christ came to set us free indeed (John 8:36).

We who were dead are now alive in Christ, and we need not fear because we are children of the most high God through the blood of His beloved Son.

Jesus ultimately conquered Satan through His death, burial, resurrection, and ascension. The great confrontation took place in the heavenly realm above the earth. There is nothing to indicate that Jesus conquered Satan while in hell. Lucifer was cast down to the earth when he led the heavenly insurrection against God. The New Testament refers to Satan as "the ruler of this world" (John 12:31) and "prince of the power of the air" (Ephesians 2:2). Clearly, Hebrews 10:12 and Ephesians 1:19-23 show that Christ took His seat at the Father's right hand in the heavenly realm.

> ### Read The Following Passage And Fill In The Blanks
> #### COLOSSIANS 2:13-15
>
> "And you, being _____ in your trespasses and
>
> the uncircumcision of your flesh, He has made _____
>
> together with Him, having forgiven you _____
>
> trespasses, {14} having _____ out the handwriting of
>
> requirements that was against us, which was contrary to us. And He has taken it out of
>
> the way, having _____ it to the cross. {15} Having
>
> disarmed principalities and _____, He made a
>
> public spectacle of them, _____ over them in it."

Although Satan has been stripped of authority, he still has the ability to steal, kill, and destroy. Satan and his demons continue to inhabit the earth and its atmosphere. Our adversary is still the "accuser of the brethren" as he has been since his banishment from heaven.

"And the LORD said to Satan, "From where do you come?" So Satan answered the LORD and said, "From going to and fro on the earth, and from walking back and forth on it."
Job 1:7

"Then I heard a loud voice saying in heaven, "Now salvation, and strength, and the kingdom of our God, and the power of His Christ have come, for the accuser of our brethren, who accused them before our God day and night, has been cast down. {11} "And they overcame him by the blood of the Lamb and by the word of their testimony, and they did not love their lives to the death."
Revelation 12:10-11

In order for us to live above the lies of the enemy, we must understand who we are in Christ. It is vital for us to understand spiritual warfare and how to use the keys of the kingdom that will direct us into victory and success. These topics will be discussed in future lessons.

Read The Following Passage And Fill In The Blanks
1 Peter 5:8-9

"Be sober, be vigilant; because your _____ the devil

walks about like a roaring lion, seeking whom he may _____ ,

{9} _____ him, steadfast in the faith, knowing that

the same sufferings are experienced by your brotherhood in the world."

We must not allow our adversary the opportunity to devour our lives, families, and blessings that God sent Christ to provide.

We Are "IN" Christ

The phrase "in Christ" is used over eighty times in the New Testament. It is important for us to realize that Christ is not only in us, we are in Him.

Acts 17:28(a) says, "for in Him we live and move and have our being..."

Here is just a sampling of other passages that make reference to our position in Christ: Romans 8:1; 1 Corinthians 1:30; 2 Corinthians 2:14, 5:17; Ephesians 2:6, 13.

"But now in Christ Jesus ye who sometimes were far off are made nigh by the blood of Christ." *Ephesians 2:13, King James Version*

Apostle Paul made very clear our position when writing to the Ephesians. He said we are seated with Christ in heavenly places (Ephesians 2:6). This is the position of victory, far above the adversary. We are to assume our place with Christ, where He is seated above all powers and principalities of the earth. This is obviously an advantageous position in strategic warfare!

Jesus Christ is alive forever and will reign in eternity. We who are "in Christ" are to rule and reign with Him (Romans 5:17). New Testament believers are referred to as kings and priests (Revelation 1:6).

Read The Following Passage And Fill In The Blanks
REVELATION 5:10

"And have made us _____ and _____ to our God;

And we shall _____ on the earth."

Believers are to rule in this life as well as in the life to come. It is only when God's people find their true identity in Christ (i.e., His death, burial, resurrection, and ascension), that they truly overcome the evil one in this life.

As a result of all that Christ has obtained on our behalf, we are able to overcome in this life and live victoriously.

"For whatever is born of God overcomes the world. And this is the victory that has overcome the world; our faith."   *1 John 5:4*

Following are some of the blessings that belong to us through the new birth:
 ♦ Power to be righteous (1 John 2:29)
 ♦ Actual adoption or "sonship" (Galatians 3:26)
 ♦ Freedom from sin (Romans 6:18)
 ♦ Love for the brethren (John 13:35)
 ♦ Love for God (John 14:21)
 ♦ Power to keep God's commandments (1 John 2:3)
 ♦ Power to overcome the world (1 John 4:4)
 ♦ Freedom from Satan (Romans 16:20)

We have received delegated authority from Christ. In other words, He has given us power of attorney to use His name and walk in victory.

"Behold, I give you the authority to trample on serpents and scorpions, and over all the power of the enemy, and nothing shall by any means hurt you."
Luke 10:19

All power in heaven and on the earth was Christ's to give. This was a totally legal action on the part of our Lord. One result of the resurrection and ascension of Christ is evident in His having authority to send the Holy Spirit, to raise up His followers, and to crown them in the kingdom of endless glory. The same authority is seen in the ability to convert sinners; to sanctify, protect, and perfect His Church; to subdue all nations to Himself; and finally, to judge all mankind.

"And Jesus came and spoke to them, saying, "All authority has been given to Me in heaven and on earth."   *Matthew 28:18*

If Jesus Christ was not equal with the Father, could He have claimed this equality of power without being guilty of insubordination and blasphemy? Surely not.

Does He not, in the fullest manner, assert His Godhead and His equality with the Father by claiming and possessing all the authority in heaven and on the earth? Yes, He does!

Jesus is the Lord.

> *"I am the Alpha and the Omega, the Beginning and the End," says the Lord, "who is and who was and who is to come, the Almighty."*   Revelation 1:8

Look up

Save —

Saved

Salvation —

PART 2

WHAT JESUS IS DOING NOW

Jesus As Savior

Sometimes we may wonder what Jesus is doing now that He has finished His mission on the earth. In this section, the goal is to bring clear understanding in regard to where Jesus is and what He is doing today on behalf of all believers. The Lord really is actively involved on our behalf. This is true regardless of whether or not we see Him, feel His presence, or hear His voice. The Bible says, "For there is one God and one Mediator between God and men, the Man Christ Jesus" (1 Timothy 2:5), and the Lord's work as Mediator is still active today.

Let's look briefly at the present day ministry of our Lord Jesus Christ. First, and perhaps foremost, Christ is our Savior.

No destruction

Read The Following Passage And Fill In The Blanks
JOHN 3:16-17

"For God so ___LOVED___ the world that He ___GAVE___

His only begotten Son, that whoever ___BELIEVE___ in Him should not

___Perish___ but have everlasting ___life___.

{17} "For God did not send His Son into the world to ~~scribbled~~

the world, but that the world through Him might be ___Saved___."

Greek

life — ZOE

World — Cosmos

To *believe in Jesus* means "to trust in, cling to, and rely on Jesus." Those who believe in Christ are saved. The word *saved* means "to heal, preserve, and make whole." In addition, Christ is our "life-giver." The adversary comes to destroy life; Jesus came to give it. //

Read The Following Passage And Fill In The Blanks
JOHN 10:10

"The _____enemy_____ does not come except to _____steal_____,

and to _____kill_____, and to _____destroy_____. I have

come that they may have _____life_____, and that they may have it

more _____abundantly_____."

The word *life*, as used in the Scripture above, is more than life as we know and understand it. The Greek word *zoe* means "life." It also refers to the absolute fullness of life that belongs to God. It is God's quality of life. This is exactly what Christ came to provide. In fact, to make the point clear, Jesus said He came that we might have this life in abundance. This is the only way that we, as believers, can rule in this world where we are living.

Jesus As High Priest

The present ministry of Christ also involves His acting as our High Priest (Hebrews 2:17; 9:11-12). This role speaks of representation before the throne of God. Jesus represents us in heaven, and we represent Him on the earth. Through His blood and by His name, we have access to the Holy of Holies, the Most Holy Place.

> *"Let us therefore come boldly to the throne of grace, that we may obtain mercy and find grace to help in time of need."* Hebrews 4:16

Of course, this is all part of the better covenant based on better promises that God makes available in the New Testament. The benefits really are astounding when we think about it. Because Christ is seated at the right hand of Majesty, we have the ability to enter and stand before the throne of the Creator. We do this boldly, but with humility, understanding that it is only through Christ that this could be accomplished.

Something else that must be pointed out: There is still no other name by which man can be saved (Acts 4:12).

The name of Jesus has the power to deliver and save the worst of souls.

Jesus As Mediator

Jesus is not only our Mediator; He is our Intercessor. This means He stands in for us and speaks on our behalf. Scripture says that Jesus actually lives to make intercession for those who come to God (Hebrews 7:25). This brings us to a further point. The Lord is our Advocate (1 John 2:1-2). Again, this refers to one who stands and speaks on behalf of another. Christ pleads our case when we fall short and acknowledge our sins and failures.

Apostle Paul referred to Christ as the source of strength.

Read The Following Passage And Fill In The Blanks
PHILIPPIANS 4:13

"I can do _____ things through _____

who _____ me."

Later, in the same chapter, Paul made reference to Jesus being the avenue through which God's provision flowed.

"And my God shall supply all your need according to His riches in glory by Christ Jesus." *Philippians 4:19*

Above everything, we must value the fact that Jesus Christ is the Lord. He is faithful and true (Revelation 19:11). He is the King of kings and the Lord of lords.

"Jesus Christ is the same yesterday, today, and forever." *Hebrews 13:8*

PART 3

THE NAME OF JESUS

Every Knee Shall Bow

Basic understanding of the power and authority made available to all believers through faith in the name of Jesus Christ is essential to living in victory. There is simply no name greater than the name of Jesus in the entire universe. There is coming a day when every knee in heaven, on the earth, and even beneath the earth will bow in reverence to our King. In that day, every tongue will confess that Jesus Christ truly is Lord, even those who did not serve Him during their life on the earth. The Creator of all things has seen fit to invest all power into this wonderful name.

"That at the name of Jesus every knee should bow, of those in heaven, and of those on earth, and of those under the earth, {11} and that every tongue should confess that Jesus Christ is Lord, to the glory of God the Father."

Philippians 2:10-11

Authority In His Name

Many Christians really do not comprehend the awesome power and authority that rests in the name of Jesus. Some do not seem to realize that God has made available this spiritual authority to as many as believe and exercise faith in His name. We know that He has all power. What we must understand is that Christ has given us the "power of attorney" to use His name. This is a legal term that simply means we have full authorization to conduct business on behalf of one who has delegated us to represent Him. It is similar to the situation of when an individual goes away and is not present to conduct business transactions. That person can have a signed and notarized document prepared by which they legally designate another individual to act on their behalf. The one who receives this delegated authority can make decisions and take action just as if the absent party was the one doing the business. Do we understand what this means? Just before Jesus Christ ascended to be with the Father in heaven, He authorized those who believe in His name to conduct business on this earth on His behalf. That means those who believe walk in the same power and authority as Christ did when He was on the earth. Remember, Jesus is in heaven representing us before the throne. Believers are on the earth representing Christ. This is really what the Great Commission is all about.

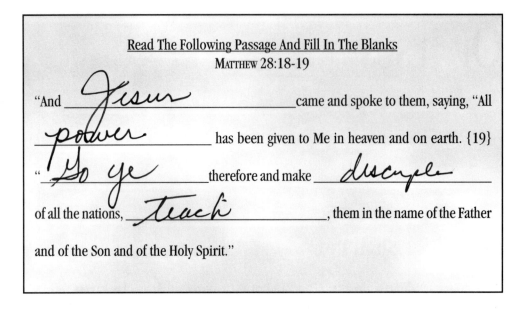

Read The Following Passage And Fill In The Blanks
MATTHEW 28:18-19

"And _____*Jesus*_____ came and spoke to them, saying, "All _____*power*_____ has been given to Me in heaven and on earth. {19} "_____*Go ye*_____ therefore and make _____*disciple*_____ of all the nations, _____*teach*_____, them in the name of the Father and of the Son and of the Holy Spirit."

All power and authority that Jesus Christ possesses is in His name. After His death, burial, and resurrection, He returned to His place in heaven. Before He departed, He promised to endue His followers with power to carry on the work of the kingdom here on the earth.

Jesus gave us power of attorney, or use of His name, for the following reasons:
   ♦   Pray with results.
   ♦   Bring salvation to the lost.
   ♦   Cast out demons.
   ♦   Minister healing.

We must remember that Christ gave us unqualified use of His name.

Faith is the channel through which grace flows; the name of Jesus is the key. Believers are the ones to whom Christ has granted His authority to act as His agents on the earth.

Prayer In Jesus' Name Receives Special Attention

"And in that day you will ask Me nothing. Most assuredly, I say to you, whatever you ask the Father in My name He will give you. {24} "Until now you have asked nothing in My name. Ask, and you will receive, that your joy may be full."
John 16:23-24

Scripture does not teach us to pray to God, "if it be Thy will"; rather, we are instructed to pray in the name of Jesus Christ, expecting to receive because we ask according to God's will.

Read The Following Passage And Fill In The Blanks
1 John 5:14-15

"Now this is the _____ that we have in _____,

that if we ask _____ according to His _____,

He hears us. {15} And if we _____that He hears us,

whatever we ask, we _____that we have the petitions that

we have _____ of Him."

This power of attorney sets the "legal" foundation for prayer. As we pray in His name, our requests pass out of our hands, and Christ assumes responsibility. He takes our place before the Father. In other words, Jesus says, "Ask the Father in My name, and I will endorse it, and the Father will give it to you." We know that the Father always hears Jesus, and when we pray in Jesus' name, it is as though Jesus Himself was praying, He takes our place. This places prayer not only on legal grounds, but makes it a business proposition. When we pray, we are taking Jesus' place here, carrying out His will, and He takes our place before the Father. Of course, the purpose for all of this is that the Father might be glorified (John 14:13).

We should know the will of the Father, ask, and have confidence that He hears and responds when we ask in the name of Jesus. When Jesus gave us the legal right to use His name, the Father knew all the name would imply when breathed in prayer. It is the Father's joy to recognize the name of Jesus. The possibilities contained in this proposition are beyond our comprehension. He is basically giving the Church a signed check on the resources of heaven and asking us to fill it in. It would serve us well to study the resources of Christ in order to get the full measure of wealth available to believers through His name.

The Name Of Jesus Used In Combat Against Forces Of Evil

In Mark 16:17-18, Jesus clearly stated that signs would follow those who believe in His name. This should not require a lengthy explanation. Either Jesus meant what

He said and said what He meant, or He did not. If He did not mean what He said here, how would we be expected to believe anything else?

The source of our power and authority is found in the name of Jesus Christ; this cannot be stressed enough. It is not in our own name, ability, or authority that we go and do these works. It is in Jesus' name and for the glory of God!

The first sign Jesus said would follow those who believe in His name was, "they will cast out demons" (Mark 16:17). In other words, they shall exercise authority over demons. Acts 16:16-18 gives the account of Apostle Paul casting a demon out of a girl who was possessed. Notice that Paul did not speak to the girl. He spoke to the spirit. He said, "I command you in the name of Jesus Christ to come out of her." The result was that the demon departed.

It might seem from reading modern religious literature and listening to the average popular preacher that demons no longer exist. However, such is not the case! Believers are to exercise spiritual authority over powers of darkness. The source of that power is faith in the name of Jesus.

There is another interesting aspect to all of this. The Lord taught His disciples in regard to the power of agreement.

Read The Following Passage And Fill In The Blanks
MATTHEW 18:19-20

"Again I say to you that if two of you ___Shall Agree___ on earth

concerning ___Any thing___ that they ___Shall Ask___,

it will be done for them by My Father in heaven. {20} "For where two or three are

___Gathered___ together in My ___NAME___,

I am there in the midst of them."

This would clearly seem to indicate that when two believers know something is the will of God, they can come into agreement and pray in the name of Jesus Christ expecting the desired result. This is what is meant by the prayer of agreement, and it is one reason that our adversary causes so much division in relationships among Christians. This is especially true in marriages, families, and churches.

The More Excellent Name

Jesus Christ has been granted what the Bible refers to as a "more excellent name" (Hebrews 1:4). There are at least three ways to obtain a great name:
- Born to a great name (such as kings)
- Through achievements
- Because it was conferred (given, awarded, bestowed)

In the case of Jesus Christ, His more excellent name came through each of these avenues.

To be sure, He inherited a great name (Hebrews 1:4). However, it is important to remember that Jesus' name is also great because of His achievements.

Read The Following Passage And Fill In The Blanks
COLOSSIANS 2:15

"Having _____ principalities and powers, He made a public

spectacle of them, _____ over them in it."

Only Christ can lay claim to this accomplishment. Only Christ conquered hell, death, and the grave!

Then there is the third way in which to obtain a great name. The name of Jesus is great because it was conferred upon Him.

"Therefore God also has highly exalted Him and given Him the name which is above every name, {10} that at the name of Jesus every knee should bow, of those in heaven, and of those on earth, and of those under the earth, {11} and that every tongue should confess that Jesus Christ is Lord, to the glory of God the Father." *Philippians 2:9-11*

Name Above All Names

God not only gave Christ a name before which every being in three worlds must bow and confess His lordship (Philippians 2:10), but also seated Him in the highest place in the universe and made Him to be Head of all things (Ephesians 1:19-22).

This was for the benefit of the Church and to fulfill God's ultimate plan for the ages. Now we know that all things have been placed under His feet. Remember, Jesus is the Head; we are the Body. Whatever is under His feet is supposed to be under ours as well. As believers in Christ, we have been raised up together with Him in heavenly places.

"But God, who is rich in mercy, because of His great love with which He loved us, {5} even when we were dead in trespasses, made us alive together with Christ (by grace you have been saved), {6} and raised us up together, and made us sit together in the heavenly places in Christ Jesus, {7} that in the ages to come He might show the exceeding riches of His grace in His kindness toward us in Christ Jesus."   *Ephesians 2:4-7*

Do All Things In His Name

As disciples of Jesus Christ, we are to do all things in His name.

If we have put faith in Christ for our salvation, we have been washed, sanctified, and justified in His name.

"And such were some of you. But you were washed, but you were sanctified, but you were justified in the name of the Lord Jesus and by the Spirit of our God."   *1 Corinthians 6:11*

We are to even give thanks to God in the wonderful name of Jesus, His Son (Ephesians 5:20). We are to pray for the sick and anoint them with oil in His name (James 5:14).

THE BLOOD OF JESUS

Sinless Blood

As believers, we should be aware of the reasons why the blood of Jesus was absolutely needful to bring about our redemption. We should develop a greater appreciation for Christ's shed blood, and thus, not "trample" it underfoot. What was so special about Jesus' blood? Why was it the only element that had power to cleanse man's sin? These are questions that are relative and important to our faith.

Jesus' blood was unique in many ways. The most profound aspect is seen in the fact that the Christ child was conceived in Mary's womb by the Holy Spirit, not by a man. If we can comprehend this truth, it will help us to better discern the blood of Jesus.

Man's lineage is determined primarily by the father's bloodline. No matter how good a man Joseph was, he could never have had perfect blood in his veins because he was born from man. Sin was in the blood of mankind by virtue of the fall of our first father, Adam. From generation to generation, sin was passed down and could be traced back to the Garden of Eden. God had a perfect plan for the redemption of mankind. The Holy Spirit came and hovered over the Virgin Mary, and Jesus Christ was conceived. Perfect blood was formed within a pure womb. The result was the perfect man, Jesus. In fact, from a scientific point of view, the blood of the mother does not have access to the child during the gestation period as a baby develops during pregnancy. Nutrients are able to pass through the placenta, and the blood flows around the child; it does not go into the child's veins. This is a very powerful and significant point. It is this truth that deems Jesus' blood perfect and free from sin.

"And according to the _____ almost all things are

_____ with blood, and without shedding of

_____ there is no _____."

Life Is In The Blood

Before we can fully understand the blood of Jesus, we must have a clearer comprehension regarding blood in general. The Bible speaks concerning the importance of blood.

> *"For the life of the flesh is in the blood, and I have given it to you upon the altar to make atonement for your souls; for it is the blood that makes atonement for the soul."*
> *Leviticus 17:11*

Blood is the only thing that has ever been able to provide atonement for man's sin. This is due to the fact that "the life is in the blood." Even in the Old Testament, when animals were being sacrificed, it was always about the blood. Without shedding of blood, there could be no covering for the transgressions of mankind. Because the life of any animal or man is found in the blood, God said it was not to be consumed. Life is sacred in God's eyes.

> *"For it (blood) is the life of all flesh. Its blood sustains its life. Therefore I said to the children of Israel, 'You shall not eat the blood of any flesh, for the life of all flesh is its blood. Whoever eats it shall be cut off."*
> *Leviticus 17:14*

Under the old covenant, the blood of animals provided atonement. It is important to understand that *atonement* simply means "to cover or appease." In simple terms, man's sin could be covered, and God could be appeased through the shedding of certain animals' blood. If we think about it, this began back in the garden where animals were sacrificed to provide a covering for Adam and Eve (Genesis 3:21). Throughout the centuries and in many cultures, blood has carried unique attributes.

The Blood Speaks

Let's consider the story of Cain and Abel. In this account, we see something very powerful and noteworthy. The two brothers each brought their offerings to the

Lord. Cain presented fruit from the ground; Abel brought the firstborn of his flock (Genesis 4:3-5).

God respected Abel's offering, but did not respect Cain's. This angered Cain, and he ended up killing his own brother. Afterward, God came looking for the murderer and said something very profound.

"And He said, "What have you done? The voice of your brother's blood cries out to Me from the ground."   *Genesis 4:10*

God said that the blood of Abel cried out to Him from the ground. The life is in the blood.

Read The Following Passage And Fill In The Blanks
HEBREWS 12:24

"To Jesus the _____ of the _____

covenant and to the _____ of sprinkling that

_____ better things than that of _____."

It is precisely because "the life is in the blood" that the blood speaks out. Think about this: Jesus' perfect and sinless blood was poured out onto the earth. This was the same dust from which the original man was formed and created by God in the beginning. Jesus' blood is now seen crying out on behalf of redemption for sinful mankind.

Another significant point in regard to our Savior's blood is seen in the fact that it was used to ratify a new and better covenant. This may help us to understand the importance of the communion elements in the New Testament Church. The bread we eat is symbolic of the flesh of Christ. The cup of juice represents His sinless blood.

"And as they were eating, Jesus took bread, blessed and broke it, and gave it to the disciples and said, "Take, eat; this is My body." {27} Then He took the cup, and gave thanks, and gave it to them, saying, "Drink from it, all of you. {28} "For this is My blood of the new covenant, which is shed for many for the remission of sins."   *Matthew 26:26-28*

Jesus said His blood was shed for the remission of sins. This is powerful because *remission* means "pardon, deliverance, forgiveness, and liberty." Under the old covenant, man did not experience deliverance and liberty from sin. The blood of animals simply acted as a covering for sin. When Jesus spoke of His blood providing remission, He spoke of man being delivered and set free from the bondage of sin.

"And according to the law almost all things are purified with blood, and without shedding of blood there is no remission."   *Hebrews 9:22*

Justified By His Blood

Today, we do not only have forgiveness for sin. We have been declared "not guilty" by virtue of the blood of Jesus Christ, the Lamb of God.

"Much more then, having now been justified by His blood, we shall be saved from wrath through Him."   *Romans 5:9*

According to definition, to be *justified* means "to be found innocent." It means that we are seen as being righteous, free from the bondage of sin. In addition, man can now live in peace with his Creator. How does anyone receive such justification?

Read The Following Passage And Fill In The Blanks
Romans 5:1

"Therefore, having been _____ by faith, we have

_____ with God through our Lord Jesus Christ,"

Everything leads back to the blood of Jesus Christ. This includes our justification and peace with God who is holy. Christ shed His innocent blood in order to reconcile man back to God.

"For it pleased the Father that in Him all the fullness should dwell, {20} and by Him to reconcile all things to Himself, by Him, whether things on earth or things in heaven, having made peace through the blood of His cross."
Colossians 1:19-20

The blood of Christ is so powerful that even our sin-filled conscience can be purged and cleansed.

"How much more shall the blood of Christ, who through the eternal Spirit offered Himself without spot to God, cleanse your conscience from dead works to serve the living God?"   *Hebrews 9:14*

Christ Purchased The Church With His Blood

The Lord paid the full purchase price for the New Testament Church. In essence, there was a price on our heads. The penalty for sin is death (Romans 6:23). There was only one way the price could be paid to redeem sinful man to a God who is described as "holy, holy, holy."

> *"Therefore take heed to yourselves and to all the flock, among which the Holy Spirit has made you overseers, to shepherd the church of God which He purchased with His own blood."*   *Acts 20:28*

By virtue of the fact that the Church, the Body of Christ, has been purchased with the blood of Christ, even our own bodies belong to God.

Read The Following Passage And Fill In The Blanks
1 CORINTHIANS 6:19-20

"Or do you not know that your _____ is the temple of the

Holy Spirit who is in you, whom you have from God, and _____

are not your own? {20} For you were _____ at

a price; therefore glorify God in your body and in your spirit, which are

_____."

As believers and followers of the Lord Jesus Christ, we need to understand that we have been redeemed through His blood. To **redeem** means "to pay a ransom." A ransom is the price paid before someone who is being held captive is set free. When a ransom is paid, it means the release has been obtained by the paying of a set price and the one in captivity is now granted liberty.

> *"Knowing that you were not redeemed with corruptible things, like silver or gold, from your aimless conduct received by tradition from your fathers, {19} but with the precious blood of Christ, as of a lamb without blemish and without spot."*   *1 Peter 1:18-19*

Knowing that we have been saved and cleansed from all sin is absolutely vital to our success as Christians. When the "accuser of the brethren" comes to remind us of our past, we must remind him of the power of Christ's blood! It is essential that we understand that the blood cleanses us from all sin.

Read The Following Passage And Fill In The Blanks
1 John 1:7

"But if we walk in the _____ as He is in the light, we

have _____ with one another, and the _____

of Jesus Christ His Son cleanses us from _____ sin."

Here we see the importance of walking in "the light" and continuing to fellowship with others of like, precious faith.

Several passages in the book of Revelation refer to the power of the blood. These include Revelation 1:5; 5:9; 7:14; and 12:11.

In conclusion, let's review some of the many benefits found in the blood of Jesus:
- The blood cleanses (1 John 1:7).
- The blood backs Christ's promises (Luke 22:20).
- The blood redeems from sin and sickness (Isaiah 53:4-6; Matthew 8:17).
- The blood gives access to God's presence (Hebrews 4:16; Hebrews 10:19).
- The blood helps us do God's will (Hebrews 9:14; 13:20-21).
- The blood overcomes Satan (Revelation 12:11).
- The blood gives safety and protection (Exodus 12:21-23).
- The blood reconciles (Ephesians 2:13-16; Colossians 1:20).
- The blood speaks for us (Hebrews 12:24).

The most powerful weapons made available to the New Testament believer are the name of Jesus, the blood of Jesus, and the Word of God. When used effectively, these three guarantee our success and victory in life.

One final word: We must guard against taking the blood of Jesus for granted or treating it with disregard.

"Of how much worse punishment, do you suppose, will he be thought worthy who has trampled the Son of God underfoot, counted the blood of the covenant by which he was sanctified a common thing, and insulted the Spirit of grace?"
Hebrews 10:29

LESSON SUMMARY

TAKE A MOMENT AND CONSIDER WHAT CHRIST HAS DONE FOR US. HE NOT only shed His sinless blood to purchase our redemption, but also went to the very pit to fully pay the penalty we deserve. He then ascended to the right hand of glory where He ever lives to make intercession on our behalf. The Lord has given believers full access to His name, which has the backing of heaven and all authority. Jesus continues His present-day ministry as High Priest, Advocate, and Mediator on our behalf. If we would only open our hearts and begin to comprehend the fullness of the inheritance that is ours in Christ, there would not be defeat or failure. We must learn to exercise the authority that Christ has bestowed to us as His followers. This involves full use of His name. The Lord has given believers absolute privilege to use His name the same as with any power of attorney. We must also walk in greater understanding of His blood. The shed blood of Christ purchased our salvation, deliverance, healing, and life. We are now the redeemed saints of God, no longer sinners filled and bound by darkness. Knowing Jesus, what He has done, is doing, and will do is a tremendous blessing and advantage in this life. Walking in His delegated authority brings great success. We must assume our God-given position with Christ "in heavenly places" (Ephesians 2:6) in order to experience the fullness of our inheritance on the earth. We need not wait to get to heaven in order to begin experiencing the good life that Christ came to purchase for us.

> *"The thief does not come except to steal, and to kill, and to destroy. I have come that they may have life, and that they may have it more abundantly."*
>
> *John 10:10*

Eternal life is ours today. When we walk in the full understanding of knowing Jesus, we walk in our God-given identities as sons and daughters of the most high God. Knowing Jesus means we understand we are not forsaken, abandoned, rejected, dejected, or cursed. We understand that we are blessed, called, appointed, accepted, and anointed to do the work of the ministry.

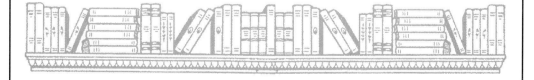

QUESTIONS *for* REVIEW

1. What was the reason that Jesus' suffering and death pleased the Father?

   _____

   _____

   _____

2. Did Christ come to do away with the Law or to fulfill it?

   fulfill it. Matthew 5:17

   _____

3. Did Christ actually become sin for us when He hung upon the cross?

   yes 2 Cor 5:21

4. When Jesus died on the cross, something very significant took place. What was torn in two?

   a. Heaven
   b. Satan
   c. Veil ⟵ *(circled)*

5. Jesus is our High Priest.

   (True)   False

6. List some of the blessings that belong to us through the new birth.

    _____

    _____

    _____

    _____

    _____

7. As found in John 10:10, what is Satan's main objective?

    a. Steal
    b. Kill
    c. Destroy
    d. All of the above

8. The source of our power and authority is found in the name of Jesus.

    True   False

9. Jesus was conceived at the consummation of Joseph and Mary's marriage.

    True   False

10. The most powerful weapon made available to the New Testament believer today is the ability to acquire wealth and recognition.

    True   False

PRAYING, JOURNALING, AND FASTING

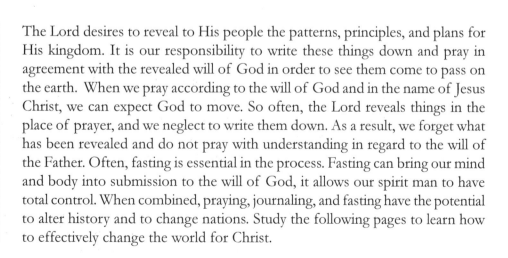

""If My people who are called by My name will humble themselves, and pray and seek My face, and turn from their wicked ways, then I will hear from heaven, and will forgive their sin and heal their land."

2 Chronicles 7:14

The Lord desires to reveal to His people the patterns, principles, and plans for His kingdom. It is our responsibility to write these things down and pray in agreement with the revealed will of God in order to see them come to pass on the earth. When we pray according to the will of God and in the name of Jesus Christ, we can expect God to move. So often, the Lord reveals things in the place of prayer, and we neglect to write them down. As a result, we forget what has been revealed and do not pray with understanding in regard to the will of the Father. Often, fasting is essential in the process. Fasting can bring our mind and body into submission to the will of God, it allows our spirit man to have total control. When combined, praying, journaling, and fasting have the potential to alter history and to change nations. Study the following pages to learn how to effectively change the world for Christ.

PART 1

PRAYING

Prayer Changes me
beholding God
become intermite

The Importance Of Prayer

As a new believer in Christ, it is essential to become and remain keenly aware of the importance and value of effectual prayer. We must continually be cognizant of our need to pray and knowledgeable in regard to various types of prayer spoken of in Scripture.

"Prayer is the most wonderful act in the spiritual realm as well as a most mysterious affair."
Watchman Nee

Jesus said we ought to "always pray and not lose heart" (Luke 18:1). That being said, we would do well to learn how to pray effectively to see God's will fulfilled. Our Lord illustrated a life of prayer and taught His disciples how to pray. In this lesson, we will examine what prayer is, why we should pray, how to pray, and hindrances to prayer. We will look at the "Lord's Prayer" as a model as well as other prayer guides.

In 2 Chronicles 7:14, we see the shared responsibility of prayer. Our part, as God's people, is to come humbly to the Lord and pray. As we seek His face and turn from our sin, God promises to hear, forgive, and heal in response to prayer.

Read The Following Passage And Fill In The Blanks
2 CHRONICLES 7:14

"If My ___children___ who are called by My name will ___humble___

themselves, and ___Seek___ and ___prayer___ My face,

and ___turn___ from their wicked ways, then I will ___hear___

from heaven, and will _____ their sin and

___heal___ their land."

Walk & Pray in the spirit

What Is Prayer?

Prayer is simply communicating with God and involves speaking as well as listening.

The words *prayer* (noun) and *pray* (verb) are found over 106 times in the New Testament. They involve action and discipline and include spending time in two-way communication with God as we give homage to Him as the Creator. As Christians, we are entitled to invoke the name of Jesus.

> *"And whatever you ask in My name, that I will do, that the Father may be glorified in the Son. {14} "If you ask anything in My name, I will do it." John 14:13-14*

Prayer is not optional for the believer in Christ. Scripture makes clear the absolute necessity for prayer. Jesus said, "when you pray," not, "if you pray" (Matthew 6:5). Apostle Paul wrote that men are to pray everywhere (1 Timothy 2:8), adding that we are to pray "without ceasing" (1 Thessalonians 5:17). *└ at all time*

(pray w/o seeking

The First Disciples Learned The Value Of Prayer

> *"And it came to pass, that, as he was praying in a certain place, when he ceased, one of his disciples said unto him, Lord, teach us to pray, as John also taught his disciples."*
> *Luke 11:1*

Jesus' disciples asked Him to teach them to pray. It is a great mistake to think that we can do it all on our own. The disciples wanted to know how Jesus could do all that He did. It is difficult to interpret at what point of Jesus' ministry the disciples approached Him with this request. By this time, according to Luke's account, they had already witnessed the following:

- A dead man who came back to life (Luke 7:15)
- People being cured of diseases and delivered from evil spirits (Luke 7:21)
- A man delivered from a legion of demons (Luke 8:30-33)
- A woman healed with one touch (Luke 8:46-48)
- The transfiguration of Moses and Elijah (Luke 9:28-31)
- Authority delegated to them over all the power of the enemy (Luke 10:19)

Matthew sets "The Lord's Prayer" at the early stage of His earthly work while Luke records this event later. Some believe it possible that Jesus had taught the principle of prayer early on, yet the disciples did not fully grasp their need for prayer until they themselves began to do the work.

"These all continued with one accord in prayer and supplication, with the women and Mary the mother of Jesus, and with His brothers."   *Acts 1:14*

Obviously, this Scripture speaks of a time later in the disciples' lives, and it was a most trying period for the followers of Christ. They were commanded to wait for something they did not understand. The dashed hopes following Jesus' crucifixion were lifted anew when Jesus rose from the dead. They knew that time was not to be wasted. They resorted to the one thing they had been taught would carry them through any situation. That one thing was prayer!

<u>Write Proverbs 15:8</u>

"The sacrifice of the wicked is an abomination to the Lord; but the prayer of the upright is his delight."

Our Attitude In Prayer

According to 2 Chronicles 7:14, we should humble ourselves in prayer. This is important because God "resists the proud but gives grace to the humble." Humility is an attitude of heart that says, "In and of myself, I can do nothing, but through Christ, I can do all things." Prayer is, therefore, an act of humility and faith.

Faith is an essential element of prayer because we cannot please God without it (Hebrews 11:6). Faith is the ability to believe God for what we do not yet see with human eyes. Scripture makes clear that when we pray we should not waver, but trust the Lord.

"Therefore I say to you, whatever things you ask when you pray, believe that you receive them, and you will have them."   *Mark 11:24*

If we believe the Bible is truly the Word of God, then we must believe that it contains the will of God, and we should pray accordingly. God's Word is His will, and His will is His Word! When we know what God's will is, we need not pray, "if it be Thy will." Scripture says we can have confidence when we pray according to God's will because He hears us and will do what we ask in Jesus' name.

Read The Following Passage And Fill In The Blanks
1 JOHN 5:14-15

"Now this is the ___Confidence___ that we have in Him, that if we ___ask___ anything according to His ___will___, He ___hears___ us. {15} And if we ___know___ that He hears us, ___what so ever___ we ask, we know that we ~~have petitions~~ have the petitions that we have asked of Him."

We know that we have whatever we ask according to God's will because He hears us when we pray in the name of His Son, Jesus Christ. Thus, we actually come to God by way of a "mediator" or "intercessor" (1 Timothy 2:5; Hebrews 7:25).

Because we have Christ, seated at the Father's right hand, we can be bold in our requests. Just think, one of the privileges we have as believers in Christ is bold access to the very throne of God. In fact, we should approach the "throne of grace" with confidence (Hebrews 4:16).

 "A Christian's prayer is a joint agreement of the will, the mind, the emotions, the conscience, and the intellect working in harmony at white heat. The body cooperates to make the prayer long enough and at a high voltage to insure tremendous supernatural results." Homer W. Hodge

Believers have the privilege of praying directly to God. The Word says we can be bold (open and blunt) in our prayers to God. James 4:2 states, "Yet you do not have because you do not ask." At the same time, verse 6 of the same chapter reminds us that, "God resists the proud, but gives grace to the humble."

Effective prayer requires both confidence and brokenness before God. We must always remember that only the blood of Jesus Christ allows us to be bold before the "throne of grace."

Handwritten margin notes:

Mark 3:35

Rom 12:2
Do not be conformed — be transformed by renewing mind

Faith to
Soul ← companion
friends
siblings
comfort
Spirit nurtured

Can be hindered in our faith depends on how raised

(I never had a natural father)

John 15:16
... God Chose me. Go + bear fruit + keep on bearing + may be lasting abide ... Ask of God gives

Fruit bearing Christian got a blank check in prayer

Jay - 15
asking - asking
& receiving

We Are To Pray Effectively

<u>Read The Following Passage And Fill In The Blanks</u>
JAMES 5:16

"_____ your trespasses to one another, and

_____ for one another, that you may be

_____. The effective, fervent _____

of a righteous man avails _____."

Effective or effectual prayer produces results. Fervent prayer is passionate prayer.

The word *effective* or *effectual* actually comes from the word from which we derive *energy* in modern English (*energeo*). The word *effectual* means "producing or able to produce the desired effect." The word *fervent* comes from the Latin word *fervere* which means "to glow showing great warmth of feeling, intensely earnest."

As we communicate freely with our heavenly Father, we can be sure that He hears us and responds as we pray according to His Word and will. Our earnest, heartfelt prayers are packed with dynamite power that is able to produce. James makes reference to Prophet Elijah, who, being an ordinary man, prayed, and God stopped the rain for 3 1/2 years. That's powerful and effective prayer!

As was previously stated, faith is an essential element of prayer that brings results. We must believe that God hears and answers when we pray. Anything less than full assurance that God hears and answers prayer is merely wishful thinking. Faith is the bedrock of our relationship with God, for it is through faith that we are even saved (Ephesians 2:8). Any and all conversations and relationships with God are built upon the foundation of faith. Prayer is first and foremost a demonstration of faith in God. The Scripture says, "But without faith it is impossible to please Him" (Hebrews 11:6).

Jesus said that if we believe, whatever we ask for, we receive (read Matthew 21:22; Mark 11:24; John 14:13-14; 16:23).

That means that our asking is another very important part of effective prayer. When we ask, we need to believe that God is able to deliver.

In the New Testament, the word *ask* actually comes from two different Greek words. The first (*erotao*) means "asking for information or making an inquiry" (John 1:19; 5:12; 16:19). The second (*aieto*) means "a desire," and includes "to call

Repeman d
Speak to
Trouble souls

Physical

for" in the definition. This term is used over seventy-five times in the New Testament!

By definition, we know that *asking* means "to call for something." We should be specific in our requests.

Remember Abraham, who in conversation with God, requested boldly, yet humbly, six times for mercy on behalf of the righteous ones in Sodom. God granted his requests (Genesis 18).

From a biblical point of view, asking does not involve begging, although asking may be emotional (Matthew 14:30). It does not involve simple hope, although what we ask may seem impossible (Luke 7:1-10). Asking does include silence or noise, though it can be in the form of a whisper or a shout (1 Samuel 1:12-13; Mark 10:47-52).

Put simply, asking does involve letting our requests be made known and expecting God to respond according to His Word and will. When we pray, we are appealing to the character and nature of God. His character is holy, and His nature is love.

As in a marriage partnership, we know God so well we can speak of His heart and pray according to His Word, will, and ways.

God does His part in accomplishing His will. He seeks a people who will love Him and walk in the calling He has placed upon their lives. This is the responsibility of the believer. God has both a plan and purpose for everyone He calls out from the world. This means us!

Jesus Is Our Example

Read The Following Passage And Fill In The Blanks
MARK 1:35

"Now in the ___*morning*___, having risen a long while before daylight,

He went out and departed to a ___*solitary*___ place; and there

He ___*prayed*___."

At the beginning of His ministry on the earth, Jesus spent a great deal of time in prayer. In fact, Scripture indicates He continued in prayer all night in regard to the selection of the original twelve apostles.

"Now it came to pass in those days that He went out to the mountain to pray, and continued all night in prayer to God. {13} And when it was day, He called His disciples to Himself; and from them He chose twelve whom He also named apostles:"   *Luke 6:12-13*

Again, Jesus is seen praying at the middle of His earthly ministry as well.

"And when He had sent the multitudes away, He went up on the mountain by Himself to pray. Now when evening came, He was alone there."Matthew 14:23

Give attention to what our Lord did. The Scripture says Jesus sent the multitude away. He went to a solitary place to be alone with the Father. It was here that Jesus found rest and meditation for the work that was ahead. Clearly, His private prayer life was the secret to His public ministry life. Through prayer, meditation, and fellowship with the Father, Jesus received the anointing to conquer all forms of wickedness and evil.

"How God anointed Jesus of Nazareth with the Holy Spirit and with power, who went about doing good and healing all who were oppressed by the devil, for God was with Him."   *Acts 10:38*

Another good example revealed at approximately the midpoint of Christ's ministry on the earth is found in the transfiguration experience. As Jesus prayed on the mount, the glory of God was manifested in tremendous fashion. While the others were sleeping, Jesus was praying. The result was that He experienced God's glory in a personal way (Luke 9:28-36).

Finally, Jesus prayed at the end of His earthly ministry.

"And He was withdrawn from them about a stone's throw, and He knelt down and prayed, {42} saying, "Father, if it is Your will, take this cup away from Me; nevertheless not My will, but Yours, be done."   *Luke 22:41-42*

This account takes place at the Garden of Gethsemane just prior to Jesus' arrest and crucifixion where He told the disciples, "Pray that you may not enter into temptation." Of course, we know that twice He found the others sleeping. It was in this place of prayer that Jesus truly "sealed the deal" and guaranteed our victory. It is significant that even at the very end of His life on the earth, Jesus prayed for the forgiveness of those who killed Him and with one final proclamation to the Father, Jesus died.

"Then Jesus said, "Father, forgive them, for they do not know what they do." And they divided His garments and cast lots."   *Luke 23:34*

"And when Jesus had cried out with a loud voice, He said, "Father, 'into Your hands I commit My spirit.' Having said this, He breathed His last."

Luke 23:46

Jesus Carries On The Ministry Of "Intercession" Today

"Therefore He is also able to save to the uttermost those who come to God through Him, since He always lives to make intercession for them."

Hebrews 7:25

By definition, the purposes for intercession are listed below:
- To come to or meet a person for any cause
- To plead the cause of others in court
- To pray for others
- To defend or vindicate another
- To commend a person
- To furnish assistance or help

The Bible reveals that the present-day ministry of Christ involves intercession for those who come to God through Him (that's us!). Now, we also have the ability and responsibility to intercede for others as well.

Jesus Teaches Us How To Pray

Read The Following Passage And Fill In The Blanks
MATTHEW 6:6-7

"But you, ___when___ you pray, go into your room, and when

you have ___closed___ your door, ___pray___

to your Father who is in the ___secret___ place; and

your Father who sees in secret will ___reward___ you openly. {7}

"And _____ you pray, do not use _____

repetitions as the heathen do. For they think that they will be heard for their

_____ words."

In days of old, most Jewish homes had a place for secret devotion. It was customary for the roofs of their houses to be flat and well-adapted for walking, conversation, and meditation. There was oftentimes a small room located on the roof of the home. Here, in secrecy and solitude, prayers could be offered, unseen by any but by any but the Lord. Jesus was simply directing His disciples to this place, or to some similar locale in order to experience communion with God.

The intent is that there should be somewhere we can be in secret, alone with God. We all need a "place" to which we can go and "shut the door"; a place where no ear will hear us but His ear, no eye will see us but His eye. Unless there is such a location, secret prayer will not be long or maintained. It is often said that we have no such place and can find none. We are away from home; we are traveling; we are among strangers; we are in cars and planes, and how can we find such seclusion?

However, the desire to pray and the love of prayer will create such places.

 "There are four things to remember when praying: God hears prayer, God considers prayer, God answers prayer, and God delivers prayer. These things cannot be repeated too often. Prayer breaks all bars, dissolves all chains, opens all prisons, and widens all straits that bind God's saints."

E. M. Bounds

Jesus had all the difficulties that we can have today, yet He practiced secret prayer. To be alone, He rose up "a long while before daylight" and went into a solitary place and prayed (Mark 1:35). For Jesus, a grove, a mountain, or a garden, provided such a place. Although He was a traveler, often among strangers and without a house, He lived in the habit of secret prayer. What excuse can we who have a home, who spend the precious hours of the morning in sleep and often refuse to practice self-denial, have for not praying and being alone with God? Our Lord would have interrupted these hours in order to escape to a solitary place so He could pray. He did it frequently. We ought to as well.

The Lord's Prayer

In what has come to be called "The Lord's Prayer," Jesus reveals truth concerning effective prayer. Though it was not His intent that we pray these exact words repetitiously, the Lord did give us a model to follow when He said, "In this manner, therefore pray."

"In this manner, therefore, pray: Our Father in heaven, Hallowed be Your name. {10} Your kingdom come. Your will be done On earth as it is in heaven. {11} Give us this day our daily bread. {12} And forgive us our debts, As we forgive our debtors. {13} And do not lead us into temptation, But deliver us from the evil one. For Yours is the kingdom and the power and the glory forever. Amen."

Matthew 6:9-13

Be consumed w/ practicing the will of God

Let's take a close look at Jesus' manner of prayer and begin to apply the principles He taught.

Our Father In Heaven, Hallowed Be Your Name

We can be bold and approach God as "our Father." At the same time, we give reverence to His various names and attributes understanding that these are manifested toward us through the blood of Jesus Christ.

The following are names and attributes of God taken from *The Covenants* by Kevin Connor and Ken Malmin:

- **Yahweh** - "I AM" (Exodus 3:14)
- **Jehovah Jireh** - "The Lord my provider" (Genesis 22:14)
- **Jehovah Rapha** - "The Lord my healer" (Exodus 15:26)
- **Jehovah Nissi** - "The Lord my banner" (Exodus 17:15)
- **Jehovah Mekaddeskum** - "The Lord who sanctifies" (Exodus 31:13)
- **Jehovah Shalom** - "The Lord my peace" (Judges 6:24)
- **Jehovah Elyon** - "The Lord most high" (Psalm 7:17)
- **Jehovah Raah** - "The Lord my shepherd" (Psalm 23:1)
- **Jehovah Tsidkenu** - "The Lord my righteousness" (Jeremiah 23:6)
- **Jehovah Shammah** - "The Lord is there" (Ezekiel 48:35)

Your Kingdom Come; Your Will Be Done On Earth As It Is In Heaven

This refers to God's will being accomplished in our personal life (including marriage, family, etc.), our church (pastor, leadership, congregation), and in our government (local, state, national).

Give Us This Day Our Daily Bread

Present specific needs to the Lord. Do not be afraid to speak of prosperity and abundance, because it is the Father's good pleasure to give us His kingdom (Luke 12:32). Be specific and fervent.

And Forgive Us Our Debts, As We Forgive Our Debtors

We shall ask for and receive forgiveness. The Bible says that God is "faithful and just to forgive us" when we confess our sins to Him (1 John 1:9).

We must also remember to forgive and release others.

And Do Not Lead Us Into Temptation, But Deliver Us From The Evil One

God cannot be tempted, nor does He tempt any man.

Relationship
1 - casual (talk about generalities)
2 - Trust (begin to speak about what think or feel)
3 - Deeptrust (share dreams, deepest part of self/inner faults)
4 - Intimacy (Psalm 46:10 - quiet self, calm, disengage + know I am God)
5 - Union (one w/ that person) God can nudge & respond

Read The Following Passage And Fill In The Blanks

JAMES 1:13

"Let no one say when he is _____, "I am tempted by

_____"; for God _____be tempted

by evil, nor does He Himself tempt_____.""

We Must Be Diligent To Put On The "Whole Armor Of God"

We should read Ephesians 6:11-18 every day if necessary. It is essential to our success and victory that we have each piece of God's protection covering our lives. It will help us as Christians to do the following:

- See Christ in each facet of the armor because He is truth, righteousness, peace, etc.
- Take into hand the "sword of the Spirit," which is the Word of God, and begin to boldly declare what it says.
- Do not be afraid or ashamed to war against powers of sin and wickedness by speaking the Word and proclaiming the blood of Jesus over our lives and families.
- Give thanks for God's "hedge of protection."

For Yours Is The Kingdom And The Power And The Glory Forever

As we pray, we should declare by faith that all needs are supplied. Thank God for provision, healing, peace, etc., and give Him thanks with praise and worship.

Effective prayer involves the following:

- Confession (acknowledge God's greatness)
- Supplication (let your requests be known unto God)
- Worship, intimacy (receive the presence of the Holy Spirit)
- Intercession (pray for others)
- Thanksgiving (for victories and prayers answered)
- Praise

As we mature in faith, we experience a desire to pray and fellowship with God. As children of God, there is a natural desire to commune with our Father. This desire can only be fulfilled when we spend time with the Lord in the place of prayer. However, we must also develop the discipline of prayer in order to grow and be strong. Prayer is a type of spiritual exercise. A degree of discipline is essential if we are going to be spiritually fit. At first, prayer may require some real work, but if we pay the price, we will achieve the next level of success. Our prayer life becomes a life of devotion to God as we spend time with Him and mature in the relationship.

Webster's Dictionary defines *devotion* as follows: "religious fervor; an act of prayer or private worship; a religious exercise or practice other than the regular corporate worship; the fact or state of being ardently dedicated and loyal."

Once we have experienced a "desire" to pray and take steps to establish spiritual "discipline," it is normal for true "devotion" and communion with God to develop.

The fourth stage in the development of an effective prayer life is "delight." Prayer actually becomes a source of great satisfaction and enjoyment. Once a believer reaches this level of maturity in prayer, they will not feel satisfied or fulfilled without a regular time of experiencing God's presence in prayer.

Desire, discipline, devotion, and delight are all elements of a successful prayer life. The desire is already in the heart of every born-again believer. God has put the desire in us. We must simply discipline ourselves to spend quality time with the Father in prayer. Discipline is necessary because we are surrounded by so many distractions. As we exercise spiritual discipline, our life becomes more fully devoted to knowing and doing the Father's will. Thus, we find great delight spending time in God's presence and experiencing effective communication with Him as the object of our delight. The time comes when we simply must spend time with our Father in order to be fulfilled on a daily basis. Prayer was a vital part of Jesus' daily life. It is also an essential part of life for the successful and overcoming Christian.

10-26

Relationship in Prayer
John 15:14+15
God Revelation is for friend so be obedient + get close.
John 10:27 Sheep hear my voice (friend of God)

James 5:15 - confess fault so one another

° My fait pleases God — earnestly seek God

John 17

PART 2

JOURNALING

Write It Down

Read The Following Passage And Fill In The Blanks
HABAKKUK 2:2

"Then the _____ answered me and said: " _____

the vision And make it _____ on tablets, That he may

run who _____ it.

Journaling has become a lost art in our society. Nearly every great man of faith has diligently recorded his walk with God. In fact, most of our Bible would be missing without someone faithfully journaling.

A journal is simply a written record of our communication with the Lord. It does not add or take away from the written Word (*logos*), but is designed to help identify God's specific Word spoken for our lives (*rhema*).

As we examine our journal entries, we will be able to discern what the Holy Spirit is saying in order to: pray more accurately, plan and track spiritual growth, study and meditate on the Word, and hear God speak in circumstances and quiet times. Journaling also helps us to reflect and look at what the Lord has done. The results are more powerful personal praise and thanks as well as a more effective witness and testimony.

It has been estimated that we forget 90-95% of what we *hear* in seventy-two hours. We forget 70% of what we *read* within seventy-two hours. We forget 50% of what we *hear* and *read* within seventy-two hours. We forget only 10% of what we *hear, read,* and *do* within seventy-two hours. But, we can remember 100% of what we *hear, read, do,* and *write*. God commanded Israel to learn His commandments by doing all four (Deuteronomy 6:5-9).

When journaling, any type of notebook or binder will meet the need.

Here are a few tips in regard to journaling:
- Be honest.
- Be persistent until consistency develops.
- Be prepared at all times to hear and record what the Spirit reveals.
- Be focused on God.

"Thus speaks the LORD God of Israel, saying: "Write in a book for yourself all the words that I have spoken to you."   *Jeremiah 30:2*

PART 3

FASTING

Purpose Of Fasting

The purpose of this lesson is to inform the believer of the various benefits derived from fasting. We will also expound on various types of biblical fasting that bring different results. Though this is a topic that is not often discussed in Christian circles, it is supposed to be a routine part of our discipleship. Jesus did not say, "if you fast," but He did say plainly, "when you fast" (Matthew 6:16-17).

Apostle Paul wrote, "for the kingdom of God is not eating and drinking, but righteousness and peace and joy in the Holy Spirit" (Romans 14:17). We live in a society that is obsessed with food and drink. As a result, people, even God's people, are often weak and suffering. This lesson will not only discuss the spiritual implications of fasting, but also the physical and emotional benefits as well.

What Is Fasting?

Fasting means "to abstain from food; to eat very little or abstain from certain foods especially for religious discipline; a period of such abstinence or self-denial."

Health Science Magazine states, "Fasting is the complete abstinence from all substances except pure water, in an environment of total rest."

> ### Read The Following Passage And Fill In The Blanks
> #### MATTHEW 6:17-18
>
> "But you, when you __fast__, anoint your head and __wash__ your face, {18} "so that you do not __appear__ to men to be __fasting__, but to your __Father__ who is in the __heaven__ place; and your Father who sees in secret will __reward__ you openly."

Again, it needs to be said, Jesus did not leave fasting open to opinion. He plainly stated, "when," not "if," leaving no doubt as to whether or not His disciples should fast. When we fast, it should not be obvious to others, nor should we seek recognition from men. The Lord said our fasting is to be unto our Father in secret. Furthermore, Jesus says we will be rewarded openly.

Fasting Facts

Dr. Alan Goldhammer gives several popular *misconceptions* people have about fasting. Here are two:
* We cannot gain strength and build resistance unless we eat.
* Food and nutrition are synonymous.

Ish 30:15-17 This say God - return to me + be saved

He adds, "As long as this illusion persists, thousands will go to premature graves."

We are not nourished by the food we eat, but in proportion to the amount we digest and assimilate. Through the ages, man has fasted and regained health, peace of mind, and a new way of life. Recently in America, there has been keen observance and interest in the positive results attained by fasting.

Fasting is as ancient as man. It is seen in every major religion and culture, even to include "fasting resorts" in America, Germany, and England where supervised fasts are conducted for health and energy.

Let's first examine some of the physical results of fasting, putting the spiritual implications aside.

Psalm 46:10 Be still and know that I am God.
106:13 Hastly forgot His ways
Isiah 26:3 Guard + keep in perfect peace = Meditate if mind stays on you.

Natural And Physical Benefits Of Fasting

For people who are trying to make permanent changes in their health and lifestyle, fasting will ease the transition. When changing to a healthier eating pattern, the body attempts to adjust physiologically by eliminating toxins, metabolic by-products, etc. When individuals try to make major dietary changes without the benefit of a fasting experience, they often run into the following symptoms:

- Fatigue
- Nausea
- Vomiting
- Diarrhea
- Joint pain
- Headaches
- Skin rashes
- Irritability
- Abdominal pain/bloating
- Depression

Fasting will often dramatically shorten the time it takes for an individual to make the transition from a conventional diet and lifestyle to the independent and energetic state associated with healthful living.

It is also very helpful when dealing with addictive lifestyles. Addiction to drugs such as alcohol, cocaine, nicotine, and caffeine are examples in which fasting can dramatically reduce the withdrawal symptoms that prevent many people from becoming drug-free. Most people are surprised at how easy it is to quit smoking or drinking with the help of fasting.

Fasting also purifies the body of toxins and impurities. We are exposed to all kinds of impurities each day. God created the human body to be self-cleansing, self-healing, and self-repairing in most cases. When properly utilized, fasting is a safe and effective means of maximizing the body's self-healing capacities. Through fasting, we give our body a physiological rest that builds energy causing it to function better.

The body uses tremendous energy to masticate, digest, assimilate, and eliminate food matter. When in a fasted state, the body directs that same energy toward the healing process rather than trying to keep up with the functions listed above. Fasting flushes the system of poison, cleanses arteries, kidneys, intestines, and all vital organs. It also allows the body's energy to concentrate on areas of greatest need. Many times when we are sick, we do not want to eat. This is nature's way of telling us to cleanse the temple!

Fasting allows the spirit to be in control of the flesh. After fasting, the mind thinks more clearly.

Fasting Is Biblical

There are many Old Testament examples of fasting.

Read The Following Passage And Fill In The Blanks

2 CHRONICLES 20:3

"And Jehoshaphat _____*feared*_____, and set himself to ___*seek*___

the LORD, and proclaimed a ___*fast*___ throughout all Judah."

It is interesting to note that this was the precise instance in Scripture where we read these words, "Do not be afraid nor dismayed because of this great multitude, for the battle is not yours, but God's. Stand still and see the salvation of the LORD" (2 Chronicles 20:15, 17).

Jehoshaphat was king of Judah. His land was coming under attack from surrounding enemy nations. Notice that Jehoshaphat "set" himself to seek God. This speaks of a diligent attitude and posture. Obviously, this leader was serious about seeking God's will and direction at this crucial point. He proclaimed a fast throughout Judah and sought the Lord earnestly. As a result, God spoke prophetically, giving specific instructions and strategy for warfare. Also, the Lord sent an encouraging word for the people.

"And he said, "Listen, all you of Judah and you inhabitants of Jerusalem, and you, King Jehoshaphat! Thus says the LORD to you: 'Do not be afraid nor dismayed because of this great multitude, for the battle is not yours, but God's."
2 Chronicles 20:15

"You will not need to fight in this battle. Position yourselves, stand still and see the salvation of the LORD, who is with you, O Judah and Jerusalem!' Do not fear or be dismayed; tomorrow go out against them, for the LORD is with you." {18} And Jehoshaphat bowed his head with his face to the ground, and all Judah and the inhabitants of Jerusalem bowed before the LORD, worshiping the LORD."
2 Chronicles 20:17-18

Other examples include:
*   Ezra proclaimed a fast that the people might humble themselves and seek God and His direction (Ezra 8:21). As a result, God answered prayer (Ezra 8:23).
*   Nehemiah humbled himself by repenting and fasting (Nehemiah 1:4). God heard his prayer, gave revelation, vision, and purpose. Doors were opened, and resources began to flow. The people turned back to God, and the Word came forth (9:1-3). Revival was the result.
*   Samuel (1 Samuel 7) called a fast that led to victory.

<u>Read The Following Passage And Fill In The Blanks</u>
1 Samuel 7:6

"So they gathered together at Mizpah, drew _____*water*_____, and

poured it out before the LORD. And they _____*fasted*_____ that day,

and said there, "We have _____*sinned*_____ against the LORD."

And Samuel judged the children of Israel at Mizpah."

God had called Samuel to lead Israel when he was a young boy. Prior to Samuel becoming a man, Israel sinned against God by misusing the Ark of the Covenant (the place of God's presence). The Lord allowed the Philistines to defeat and oppress His people. The enemy even captured the Ark from the Israelites (1 Samuel 4:17). The glory of God had departed!

In addition to Samuel's functions as prophet and priest, he was the last judge before a king (Saul) was chosen to rule Israel. Samuel united the people through revival. From the believer's perspective, Samuel's fast is seen as a fast for revival and the harvest of souls. Proper preparation for this fast:

- Recognize sinful habits, demonic oppression, memories, and hurts from the past.
- Separate from secret sin. Many times, hidden sin is revealed as we fast and spend quality time seeking God. (Remember the prodigal son: He came to himself when he was hungry!)
- Must turn from all degrees of backsliding (moving farther from God instead of closer). This is a call for sincere repentance.

If we refer back to 1 Samuel chapter 7, we will note the progression as Samuel first gathered the people together and called for corporate confession and repentance of sin (v. 6). The enemy opposes this type of action (v. 7). Samuel presents an offering to God (v. 9). God moved in a mighty way and brought victory to His people by confounding the opposing forces (v. 10). Ultimate victory was won as God's people sought the Lord and pursued the enemy with a vengeance (vv. 12-13). So, we see the consequence of clean-up, crisis, and climax resulting from repentance, restoration, and revival.

People must recognize their need for revival before they can experience it! When Samuel called the people to repent, fast, and seek God, they did so because they recognized their need. The people cried out to God in frustration and desire for deliverance. God moves through man's desperation.

<u>Read The Following Passage And Fill In The Blanks</u>
PSALM 139:23-24

" *Search* me, O God, and know my *heart* ;

Try me, and know my anxieties; {24} And see if there is any *wicked*

way in me, And lead me in the way *everlasting*

New Testament Examples

There are many New Testament examples of fasting. A few of them are listed below:

- ◆ Anna (Luke 2:36-37)
- ◆ John's followers (Matthew 9:14-15)
- ◆ Church at Antioch (Acts 13:3)
- ◆ Apostle Paul (Acts 9:9; 27:9-11; 2 Corinthians 6:5; 11:27)
- ◆ Husbands and wives are to fast (1 Corinthians 7:5)

There are also several examples of forty-day fasts mentioned in Scripture. These include the following:

- ◆ Moses (Deuteronomy 9:9)
- ◆ Elijah (1 Kings 19:8)
- ◆ Jesus (Matthew 4:2; Luke 4:2)

The purpose of the forty-day fast is obviously not simply for personal needs to be met. It is to bring about change according to God's plan and purpose. This type of fast is directed toward establishing kingdom authority and taking dominion over principalities and powers that oppose the children of God.

God's Chosen Fast

There are many souls whom the Lord wants to set free. Liberty (revival) must begin in God's house. Therefore, God's people must be free from sin, oppression, and bondage.

"Therefore if the Son makes you free, you shall be free indeed."   *John 8:36*

Believers are supposed to fast though no regulations or set rules are given as to how long or how often. Believers should fast when under chastening or judgment, in need, worried, in trouble, in spiritual conflict, or desperate in prayer. Those of great power and prayer have always routinely fasted. Prayer and fasting have preceded nearly every known recorded revival in the world.

<u>Read The Following Passage And Fill In The Blanks</u>
ISAIAH 58:6

"Is this not the _____ *fast* _____ that I have chosen: To loose the

_____ *bonds* _____ of wickedness, To undo the heavy

_____ *burdens* _____, To let the oppressed go free, And that you

break every yoke?"

Spiritual Benefits Of Fasting

We have already discussed some of the physical and emotional benefits related to fasting. Here are some spiritual benefits:

Intensified Prayer

Those who found spiritual value during times set aside for fasting and prayer are found in Scripture as well as Church history and include: Jesus Christ, Paul, Daniel, Elijah, Ezra, Esther, David, Hannah, Isaiah, and Nehemiah. Modern day leaders who have fasted include: John Calvin, Martin Luther, John Knox, John Wesley, David Brainard, George Mueller, and many others.

They discovered that abstaining from food allowed them to focus on the Lord with fresh intensity, and this opened avenues of spiritual perception and understanding that were not available during the rush of routine living. They found as they focused on God with deliberate discipline, God focused on them in clarity of direction and quickening of spirit. They could partake of God more easily with everything else laid aside.

Increased Ability To Hear Holy Spirit

The plain truth is that fasting "tunes us in" to God and enables us to hear the voice of the Spirit as He imparts knowledge and direction to us. Many times, we are making decisions and taking action without seeking God and clearly receiving His wisdom and guidance.

"So we fasted and entreated our God for this, and He answered our prayer."
Ezra 8:23

> ### Read The Following Passage And Fill In The Blanks
> #### ACTS 13:2
>
> "As they _____ministered_____ to the Lord and _____fasted_____,
>
> the Holy Spirit _____said_____, "Now separate to Me Barnabas
>
> and Saul for the work to which I have called them."

Increase Of Spiritual Power

Luke's Gospel account gives a very good example of fasting in the life of Christ. This is especially true in regard to the fourth chapter. Here we see Jesus, having been led "by the Spirit" into the wilderness (v. 1), He fasted forty days and triumphed over Satan. Afterward, we see Him returning "in the power of the Spirit" (v. 14). Is there a connection?

In verse 16, Jesus entered the synagogue (Jewish house of worship), and He read from Isaiah chapter 61. Here is what Jesus declared as He read:

> *"The Spirit of the LORD is upon Me, Because He has anointed Me To preach the gospel to the poor; He has sent Me to heal the brokenhearted, To proclaim liberty to the captives And recovery of sight to the blind, To set at liberty those who are oppressed."*
> *Luke 4:18*

It was at this time that the earthly ministry of Jesus Christ began in earnest. Later, He would teach the disciples the importance of prayer combined with fasting in order to walk in greater demonstrations of power.

> *"However, this kind does not go out except by prayer and fasting."*
> *Matthew 17:21*

Increased Intimacy With God

We must remember that the true emphasis of fasting is to draw closer to God and minister unto Him. The more we experience the Lord's presence, the more we experience peace and rest, and the more we learn of Him. The more we learn of Him, the more our faith is increased, and thus, we walk in greater spiritual authority. Faith in God is exercised and manifested through greater works for His kingdom and glory!

Fasting seems to bring personal "spiritual awakening." God is calling for His people to wake up and prepare for the harvest. The Lord is sounding the alarm to awaken His warriors. It seems that many are yet sleeping.

"How long will you slumber, O sluggard? When will you rise from your sleep?"

Proverbs 6:9

God's watchmen have not all been watching.

"His watchmen are blind, They are all ignorant; They are all dumb dogs, They cannot bark; Sleeping, lying down, loving to slumber."　　Isaiah 56:10

Clearly, it is time for the Church (Bride) to awaken and come out of the closet!

Read The Following Passage And Fill In The Blanks
JOEL 2:15

"Blow the ___Trumpet___ in Zion, Consecrate a ___fast___,

Call a _____ assembly."

The prophet goes on to speak about the move of God and revival.

"And it shall come to pass afterward That I will pour out My Spirit on all flesh; Your sons and your daughters shall prophesy, Your old men shall dream dreams, Your young men shall see visions. {29} And also on My menservants and on My maidservants I will pour out My Spirit in those days."　　Joel 2:28-29

Too many, both in the church and in the world, have been taken captive by Satan and by the lusts of their own flesh or carnal appetites (2 Timothy 2:26; James 1:14-15).

Increased Anointing

Difference between Power, Anointing

Believers will experience a greater release of the Holy Spirit's anointing as we abstain from natural desires (even food) and draw closer to God (James 4:7-10). Jesus makes clear reference to our need for fasting as it relates to deliverance (Matthew 17:14-21). He taught that certain demonic strongholds will only be broken through intense prayer and fasting. Fasting brings spiritual strength that enables us to stand and tear down enemy strongholds. Demonic activity surrounds us and attempts to hinder the move of God in our lives in areas of home, marriage, finances, and church. We must have God's sufficient grace to exercise spiritual authority over demons!

Read 2 Corinthians 10:3-6 from the New Living Translation:

"We are human, but we don't wage war with human plans and methods. {4} We use God's mighty weapons, not mere worldly weapons, to knock down the Devil's strongholds. {5} With these weapons we break down every proud argument that keeps people from knowing God. With these weapons we conquer their rebellious ideas, and we teach them to obey Christ. {6} And we will punish those who remained disobedient after the rest of you became loyal and obedient."
2 Corinthians 10:3-6, New Living Translation

Guidelines For Fasting

One of the first recommendations is that we enter into fasting with a positive attitude and faith.

Read The Following Passage And Fill In The Blanks
Hebrews 11:6

"But without _____ it is impossible to _____

Him, for he who comes to God must _____ that He is,

and that He is a rewarder of those who diligently _____ Him."

We should not wait for an emergency in order to fast. It is better to begin fasting when we are spiritually "up," not feeling low and depressed. There is a law of progress in God's kingdom: "from strength to strength" (Psalm 84:7), "from faith to faith" (Romans 1:17), "from glory to glory" (2 Corinthians 3:18).

We need not begin with too long of a fasting period. It is generally best to start by omitting a couple of meals and then move on to longer periods. This prevents discouragement. Also, if we are under a physician's care, we should seek advice. We must not start with a forty-day fast!

It would behoove us to remember, the point is to draw closer to God, so during the fast, we should give much time to Bible reading and prayer. This should be a time of fresh revelation and spiritual renewal. It is all right to set objectives in fasting. We can make a list and watch God move and faith increase.

We are to avoid boasting during times of fasting. Our lives should appear as routine and normal as possible unless we are on a prolonged fast. We should go back and read Matthew 6:16-18 again! Let us always keep a watchful eye on motives. They should be Spirit and Word inspired.

The physical body is the temple of the Holy Spirit. As we fast, we cleanse that temple! If we are on any medication, we should consult a physician.

Symptoms Of Distress

It is common to experience some symptoms of distress early in a fast. These might include: dizziness, headache, nausea, etc. We must not allow this to discourage us. Our systems are being cleansed from impurities, and our bodies are used to being in control. We must simply take authority and remain positive. Most of us are used to eating out of habit, not hunger! During a fast, many people drink only water, others partake in only juices and/or broth. Each of us must work out our own pattern as the Lord gives wisdom and direction. Purified or distilled water is recommended and can be taken with a squeeze of fresh lemon or pure honey, as these will aid in cleansing. When abstaining from all food and fluids, fasting should be limited to seventy-two hours. Any longer period can have disastrous physical effects.

Break The Fast Gradually

It is best to begin with fresh fruit and light vegetables that are easy to digest. It is very important to exercise self-control! Eating too heavy will cause discomfort. Overindulging may nullify any physical benefits. If the fast exceeds two days, the stomach will begin to shrink. Do not overindulge! Eat lightly, and the stomach will adjust itself appropriately.

Keep in mind that the digestive system has been in a state of rest. Eating foods that are difficult to digest and assimilate can cause great discomfort. This is especially true at the end of a prolonged period of fasting. Ending a forty-day fast with a heavy meal can cause a person to end up in the hospital due to the inability of the body to properly digest and eliminate food matter. Always seek God and use wisdom when fasting for extended time periods.

LESSON SUMMARY

PRAYING, JOURNALING, AND FASTING ARE ALL NECESSARY ELEMENTS OF effective Christian discipleship. When we pray with faith, believing in the name of Jesus, the blood of Jesus, and the Word of God, we can expect to see results. As we become skilled in the Scriptures and pray according to the will of the Lord, situations change and lives are restored. Hearing from God is as important as praying to God. It is vital to pay attention and take note when the Spirit of the Lord is communicating to us. The fact is, we are very prone to forget what the Lord has revealed or instructed when we fail to write things down. If we develop a systematic way to record prayer needs and requests, we are also able to track our victories. It can be very exciting to look back at things we felt God was showing us as we prayed and saw His hand at work in our lives.

> *"Then the LORD answered me and said: "Write the vision And make it plain on tablets, That he may run who reads it. {3} For the vision is yet for an appointed time; But at the end it will speak, and it will not lie. Though it tarries, wait for it; Because it will surely come, It will not tarry."*   *Habakkuk 2:2-3*

Fasting is also essential to living a victorious life in Christ. It seems obvious that Jesus expected His disciples to fast. Remember, He said, "when you fast," not "if you fast" (Matthew 6:16). To be a disciple requires discipline. Fasting is not only a form of discipline, but also a spiritual act that draws us closer to God. There are numerous health benefits to living a "fasted" life. It is very clear that all three: praying, journaling, and fasting are important elements of the normal Christian life. We need to begin today, if we have not already, to implement all three of these disciplines into our everyday lives. We should form a habit of speaking to the Lord, listening for His voice, and writing down what He says. A few minutes a day can lead to a lifetime of reward and promise.

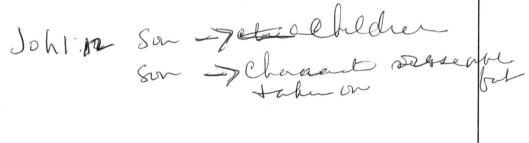

QUESTIONS for REVIEW

1. What is prayer?

   Communicaty w/ God

2. Effective prayer requires what two elements?

   Faith

   Asking

3. Name three purposes of intercession.

4. List four names of God.

   Yahweh - I am

   Jireh - my provider

   Shalom - peace

   Nissi   provider healer

   Raphas

5. God commanded Israel to learn the commandments by doing what four things?

read, hear, write, do

6. Fasting can aid people who are trying to make permanent changes in their lifestyle.

(True)　　　False

7. When properly utilized, fasting is a safe and effective means of maximizing the body's self-healing capacities.

(True)　　　False

8. Fasting can increase our spiritual power.

(True)　　　False

9. Fasting increases intimacy with God.

(True)　　　False

10. Long fasts must be broken gradually.

(True)　　　False

COMMUNION WITH GOD

"Jesus answered and said to him, "If anyone loves Me, he will keep My word; and My Father will love him, and We will come to him and make Our home with him."
John 14:23

If ever there was a time when God is bringing revelation to His Church, it is today. If ever there was time when God's people need to hear His voice, it is now. We must train ourselves to hear and hearken unto the voice of the Lord. The goal of this lesson is to help us understand how God speaks and to assist us in developing a hearing ear. We all need to know how to discern our Lord's voice and how to respond when He calls. It is also important to be aware of some hindrances to communication with the Lord. When we are well informed, nothing can prevent us from freely hearing and doing the will of God. This lesson will teach on several "keys" to experiencing God, and it is exciting to discover what they are in order to maintain open communion with our Creator. Experiencing the Lord is like no other experience we will ever have in our lives.

PART 1

HEARING GOD

Why Hearing God Is Important

God wants to fellowship and commune with us. However, fellowship is a bidirectional relationship. Could it be possible that God in heaven, the Creator of all things, really wants to speak to us individually? Yes! It is not only possible; it is true. The Lord was probably speaking to us long before we heard His voice.

Some biblical examples of communion between the Lord and man:
- God communicated with Adam and Eve in the garden.

    "And they heard the sound of the LORD God walking in the garden in the cool of the day, and Adam and his wife hid themselves from the presence of the LORD God among the trees of the garden. Then the LORD God called to Adam and said to him, 'Where are you?'"   *Genesis 3:8-9*

- God visited Abraham on His way to Sodom and Gomorrah.

    "And the LORD said, "Shall I hide from Abraham what I am doing."
    Genesis 18:17

- Enoch and Noah "walked with God" (Genesis 5:24; 6:9).

It is really true. God desires that we walk (commune and converse) with Him daily. Our relationship with God is dependent on hearing Him because relationship involves fellowship and communication.

<u>Read The Following Passage And Fill In The Blanks</u>
2 CORINTHIANS 13:14

"The _____*Grace*_____ of the Lord Jesus Christ, and the _____*love*_____

of God, and the _____*Communion*_____ of the Holy Spirit be with you all. Amen."

In the above Scripture, Paul communicates his desire for believers to experience three facets of relationship with God:

- To know the *grace* of our Lord Jesus Christ
- To know the *love* of God
- To know the *communion* of the Holy Spirit

The word *communion* means "partnership, participation, communication, and/or fellowship."

Our relationship with God determines how we hear Him. What is our motivation?

- Love of God?
- Fear of punishment?
- Hope of reward?
- Desire for selfish gain?

(disciple must continue in God's Word.)

The True Disciple Must Hear God

✓ A disciple is one who continues <u>in God's Word.</u>

"Then Jesus said to those Jews who believed Him, "If you abide in My word, you are My disciples indeed. {32} "And you shall know the truth, and the truth shall make you free." *John 8:31-32*

A disciple is also one who follows <u>Christ.</u>

"And when he brings out his own sheep, he goes before them; and the sheep follow him, for they know his voice." *John 10:4*

<u>Read The Following Passage And Fill In The Blanks</u>
JOHN 10:27

"My sheep hear My _____*voice*_____, and I _____*know*_____ them, and they

_____*follow*_____ Me."

Not just born but sent through birth, therefore have a purpose

Jesus, our example, had to hear in order to fulfill the Father's will (John 5:30).

If we do not hear and follow the voice of our Master, how can we ever hope to do what He desires? We have many choices every day; but one choice is truly needful! That is the choice to have communion with God each day.

This is very clearly seen in the Bible story about Mary and Martha (Luke 10:38-42). These were some of Christ's closest friends whom He loved and seems to have visited frequently.

Take note of Mary's position and posture. She "sat at Jesus' feet."

> *"And she had a sister called Mary, who also sat at Jesus' feet and heard His word."*
> *Luke 10:39*

Try not to minister out of a need but out of our overflow

This denotes close attention. She committed to "hang on every word" and receive all that Christ delivered. Mary sat at Jesus' feet as students sit at the feet of their tutors during interesting lectures. When we sit at Christ's feet to hear His Word, it signifies submission, a readiness to receive, and deference to His instructions. The Scripture says that Mary "heard His Word." As surely as Christ came to speak, Mary was "swift to hear" (James 1:19). We would do well to learn to listen.

Mary's sister, Martha, complained to the Lord (Luke 10:40).

Jesus' response to Martha's complaint: "Martha, Martha, you are worried and troubled about many things" (Luke 10:41). It is all too easy for us as believers to get entangled with the cares and affairs of this temporal life. We often open the door to confusion by giving place to what Jesus referred to as "the cares of this world, the deceitfulness of riches, and the desires for other things" (Mark 4:18-19).

Jesus said to Martha, "But one thing is needed, and Mary has chosen that good part, which will not be taken away from her" (Luke 10:42).

The "one thing" that is needed for the disciple of Christ is to know and hearken to the voice of the Great Shepherd. Time alone with the Lord, coupled with the ability to discern His voice, will result in good decisions when acted upon.

Preparing To Hear

There are several things we can do in preparation for hearing God.

Love The Word Of God

The Scriptures point the way to a meaningful relationship with God.

The Bible is a series of letters from the Lord that communicate His love and grace. Learning about God and His ways will prepare us to better listen to Him.

To read the Bible while ignoring the Author is offensive to the One who inspired it. To many people, the Bible is simply a book of history or law and not a Book of Life. This must surely grieve the Lord.

Read The Following Passage And Fill In The Blanks
2 TIMOTHY 3:16

"All Scripture is given by _*inspiration*_ of God, and is

profitable for _*doctrine*_, for _*reproof*_,

for _*correction*_ for _*instruction*_ in righteousness."

Ask The Holy Spirit To Reveal Christ In The Bible

Scripture tells us that the Holy Spirit is our Helper (John 14:26). He will teach us and bring things to our remembrance that we need to know in order to live a successful life. The Spirit will speak of Jesus as the "way, the truth, and the life" (John 14:6).

Develop A Listening Ear

Like children, we can learn to listen. We learn to recognize the voice of the Lord through frequency of time spent with Him, intensity of time spent with Him, and practice (trial and error).

Listening is vital! Consider the following:

"But He answered and said, "It is written, 'Man shall not live by bread alone, but by every word that proceeds from he mouth of God.'"   *Matthew 4:4*

Faith and relationship with God grow as we learn to listen.

Read The Following Passage And Fill In The Blanks
ROMANS 10:17

"So then _*faith*_ comes by hearing, and _*hearing*_

by the _*word*_ of God."

Developing a hearing ear is an act of the will, a quality decision of choice. It is important for us to remove distractions. There are some things we can do to better hear the voice of the Lord. First of all, practice the art of being still. This involves a state of waiting on the Lord. Being still cannot be hurried or forced. We must allow it to happen. This is an exercise to be learned, especially for those of the Western culture. It is the opposite of physical tension; we would do well to remember that the fourth commandment is to rest. The Bible speaks of the need for God's people to find "rest" in the Lord. We need to regularly experience physical, emotional, and mental calm (read Hebrews 3:18; 4:9-12).

Focus On The Word And The Lord

Meditation is a biblical idea, not New Age or Yoga. The opposite of focused attention could be busy distractions.

> *"This Book of the Law shall not depart from your mouth, but you shall meditate in it day and night, that you may observe to do according to all that is written in it. For then you will make your way prosperous, and then you will have good success."*
>
> *Joshua 1:8*

It would help for us to just let go of things at times. We must back off from being in control. The opposite of "letting go" could be overcontrol.

Read The Following Passage And Fill In The Blanks

PHILIPPIANS 4:6-8

"Be _Careful_ for nothing, but in everything by prayer and supplication, with thanksgiving, let your requests be made known to God; {7} and the _peace_ of God, which surpasses all understanding, will guard your hearts and minds through Christ Jesus. {8} Finally, brethren, whatever things are _true_, whatever things are _honest_, whatever things are _just_, whatever things are _pure_, whatever things are _lovely_, whatever things are of good report, if there is any _virtue_ and if there is anything praiseworthy; _Think_ on these things."

It helps if we position ourselves to receive and hear. We know what it is like to try to speak and hear at the same time. It is not possible to really listen when we are too busy talking (James 1:19, "slow to speak"). Many times, we actually do the opposite of positioning ourselves to receive through our involvement with too much activity.

It would also help if we have our Bible along with a notebook and pen. We should get in the habit of writing things down as the Lord begins to speak. We also need to do more listening than talking and allow the Holy Spirit to flow spontaneously. Another common hindrance to receiving Holy Spirit guidance is excessive analytical thought.

It may also be helpful to listen to soothing music or simply to sing songs of worship to the Lord. The point is, we must get into the Spirit and out of our carnal mindset in order to hear more clearly from God. We would do well to consider how spiritual music helped the prophet, Elisha, in preparation to hear the Lord (2 Kings 3:15).

> *Meditation leads to clear thinking.*
> *Clear thinking leads to good decisions.*
> *Good decisions result in good success.*

Normal Christianity Is To Live And Walk By The Spirit

"But you are not in the flesh but in the Spirit, if indeed the Spirit of God dwells in you. Now if anyone does not have the Spirit of Christ, he is not His."
Romans 8:9

God speaks in a variety of ways:
+ His Word
+ His Spirit
+ His leaders
+ His people
+ Life circumstances

Keep in mind that God is our Father, and He knows what is best for us. In fact, there are some 267 references to God the "Father" in the New Testament. He speaks as a father to His children.

The voice of God will always confirm the Bible. He will never violate it.

Three principles of guidance:
+ God is more interested in the development of our character than changing our circumstances (2 Corinthians 12:9).

- ◆ God deals more with attitudes and principles than He deals with behavior (Mark 7:6-7).
- ◆ God guides more with "yes/no" and "do/don't," than with reasoning. This requires faith and trust on our part.

We can actually train ourselves to hear God as we learn to rest in His presence and recognize His voice. We need to stop doubting our ability to hear. We should begin to write as the Lord speaks, and look and listen as we pray and rest. We can expect the Bible to come alive.

Read The Following Passage And Fill In The Blanks
HABAKKUK 2:2-4

"Then the LORD _answered_ me and said: " _Write_

the vision And make it plain on tablets, That he may run who _read_

it. {3} For the vision is yet for an appointed time; But at the end it will

Speak , and it will not lie. Though it tarries,

Wait for it; Because it will surely come, It will not

tarry. {4} "Behold the proud, His soul is not upright in him; But the just shall live by his

faith ."

Unbelief
disobedient

PART 2

ENCOUNTERING GOD'S PRESENCE

God Has A Purpose And Plan For Each Of Our Lives

It is the right and responsibility of every believer to seek God and allow His will to be made clear. The Scripture says, "seek, and you will find" (Matthew 7:7). It is not that the Lord is playing "I've Got A Secret"; however, He does expect and command that we earnestly search in order to understand what He is doing in the world and in our own lives.

"Draw near to God and He will draw near to you. Cleanse your hands, you sinners; and purify your hearts, you double-minded."   *James 4:8*

"And you will seek Me and find Me, when you search for Me with all your heart."   *Jeremiah 29:13*

As we earnestly seek the One who has given us life, He will reveal Himself to us in ways that we can understand. This is because the Lord desires to bring revelation to every one of His children. Knowing and doing the will of God is the only way we can live a truly successful life. We may reach a level of success according to the world's standard without having Christ at the center of our life, but we can never hope to accomplish the will and purpose of the One who put us here if we do not know how to hear from Him and experience His presence.

Read The Following Passage And Fill In The Blanks
PHILIPPIANS 2:13

"For it is _____God_____ who works in _____you_____

both to will and to do for His good _____pleasure_____."

[handwritten margin notes: Obtain Mercy / Find Grace / God forgive when we repent / Get sin out / to really experience / God's presence in / a deeper way / Exodus 3:14]

A great work has begun in each of us, and it is God who will bring it to completion as we set our hearts to follow Him (Philippians 1:6).

In the book, *Experiencing God*, the authors (Henry T. Blackaby and Claude V. King) expound on seven realities that are involved in hearing and experiencing God. We believe they are very relevant for us today. Every student is encouraged to purchase and complete the *Experiencing God* workbook during private study time.

All of us need to spend time in prayer and meditation on a regular basis in order to learn how to clearly recognize the voice of the Lord. We need to remember, Jesus said, "My sheep hear My voice, and I know them, and they follow Me" (John 10:27).

As we become more attentive to events around us, it becomes evident that God is working through circumstances and people in our lives, "both to will and to do for His good pleasure" (Philippians 2:13).

The seven points of *Experiencing God* have been used with permission. They are progressive in nature and are listed below:

1. God is always at work around us.

2. God pursues a continuing love relationship with us that is real and personal.

3. God invites you to become involved with Him in His work.

4. God speaks by the Holy Spirit through the Bible, prayer, circumstances, and the Church to reveal Himself, His purposes, and His ways.

5. God's invitation for you to work with Him always leads you to a crisis of belief that requires faith and action.

6. You must make major adjustments in your life to join God in what He is doing.

7. You come to know God by experience as you obey Him, and He accomplishes His work through you.

It may help focus to go back and carefully read each of those seven points once again. Let us meditate for a moment on each statement and how it relates to our personal lives.

The Lord can and will direct our steps as we learn to hear and obey His voice, walking by faith.

"Trust in the LORD with all your heart, And lean not on your own understanding;
{6} In all your ways acknowledge Him, And He shall direct your paths."

Proverbs 3:5-6

The issue of Lordship must also be settled in our heart and lifestyle. In addition, it helps if we remember that Jesus Christ is "the way."

Read The Following Passage And Fill In The Blanks
JOHN 14:6

"Jesus said, "I am the ___*way*___, the ___*truth*___,

and the ___*light*___. No one comes to the Father except

through ___*Me*___.""

We may take note that Jesus **did not** say, "I will show you the way. I will give you a road map. I will clearly tell you when to turn one way or the other."

He did say, "I AM the way." Jesus knows the way because He is the way. We should think about this: If we were to daily do everything the Lord tells us, would we always be in the center of God's will for our lives? The answer is yes!

As we learn to discern the voice and leading of the Lord on a daily basis, it becomes much easier to release "the way" to Him. We can do what God tells us one day at a time and know that He will give us plenty to fill each day with meaning and purpose. If we do what He says, we will be in the center of His will when He wants to use us for special purposes.

It may help to remember that it is God who has given us this life. He knows what we are able to do because He has made us the way we are. Every one of us has abilities from the Lord. Those abilities can and should be used to bring increase to His kingdom and glory to His name. The amazing thing is that God has called each of us to do things that only He can do. This is the reason that faith is required.

The Bible is full of examples of men and women the Lord used to accomplish great things. They all had to learn to hear, trust, and obey.

Trust And Obey

As believers, our greatest responsibilities are to trust and obey. This is not always as easy as it sounds. In fact, the failure to trust and obey is what ultimately caused the children of Israel to not enter the Land of Promise (Hebrews 3:18-19).

Abraham, the father of faith, learned this early on in his experience with God. When the Lord first revealed His divine will to Abram, it came as a simple command (Genesis 12:1-5). All that Abram knew was that God had given the command for him to leave where he was and go where the Lord would show him. This reveals something important for us to learn. We must be willing to follow by faith and obedience, not by sight. Abram had no one to teach him about God, yet he followed. He had no Bible. He was not filled with the Spirit as we are, yet Abram was willing to step out in obedience. Why do we have such a hard time hearing, trusting, and obeying?

Obedience *to* God does require faith *in* God. Jesus gives a very simple command to those who serve Him. In each Gospel account, He states very simply, "Follow Me." It is not possible to obey this command if we are not willing to give the Lord the throne of our life. We must set priorities and seek God instead of things.

Read The Following Passage And Fill In The Blanks
MATTHEW 6:33-34

"But _____ first the kingdom of God and His _____,

and all these things shall be added to you. {34} "Therefore do not _____

about tomorrow, for _____ will worry about its own things.

Sufficient for the day is its own trouble."

It is important to understand and agree that God is absolutely worthy of our trust. The question is, are we willing to follow Him one day at a time? Will we agree to follow Him even when He does not reveal all the details ahead of time?

If we really believe that Jesus is "the way," then we should learn to love, trust, and obey Him!

In reality, God is always at work around us. This is true wherever we go, and it has been so since the beginning of time.

Note what Jesus said:

"But Jesus answered them, "My Father has been working until now, and I have been working."   *John 5:17*

God does His part; we must do ours. Like Jesus, we must understand the need to do those things that are revealed from the Father. Jesus said, "the Son can do nothing of Himself, but what He sees the Father do" (John 5:19).

It is impossible for us to stay as we are and go on with God. Discipleship means that God is moving us from where we are to where He wants us to be. The Lord wants to reveal Himself, but we must take time to seek Him. We need to ask God to speak and make His will clear in order to lead us into true and lasting success. What is success? Simply defined, success is to know and do the will of God. We cannot be entangled with all the things of the world and experience God on a continual daily basis, nor can we be caught up with selfish ambition. Scripture warns against falling prey to the lust of the flesh, the pride of life, and the deceitfulness of riches (1 John 2:16).

It also helps to understand that the Lord rarely shows us the entire picture all at once. We must be willing to prove ourselves each step of the way.

Not only is God at work all around us, He is also pursuing a relationship with us.

Read The Following Passage And Fill In The Blanks
MATTHEW 22:37-38

"Jesus said to him, " You shall _____ the LORD your God with

all your _____, with all your _____,

and with all your _____.' {38} "This is the first

and _____ commandment."

A true love relationship involves genuine devotion to another. By definition, it involves feelings toward someone, however, it is much greater than mere human emotion. The love relationship involves a strong attachment that suggests tenderness, like that found in the parent/child or other familial relationships. There is a sense of trust and loyalty that may not be realized with everyone outside the family.

How Do We Know God Loves Us?

The answer is found throughout Scripture. Consider the following regarding God and man:

- He created us in His image (Genesis 1:27).
- He formed us in our mother's womb (Psalm 139:13).
- He loved us before we loved Him (1 John 4:19).
- He draws us to Himself (Jeremiah 31:3).

God does His part; we must do ours.

We can move closer to the Lord and make our relationship real and personal as we do the following:

- Pray (communicate).
- Read the Word (discover things about Him).
- Allow the Spirit to lead (walk with God).
- Fast and abstain from appetites of the flesh (offer a living sacrifice).

How Do We Demonstrate Love For God?

Again, the answer is found in Scripture.

Read The Following Passage And Fill In The Blanks
JOHN 14:21

"He who has My commandments and _Keepth_ them, it is he who _Loveth_ Me. And he who loves Me will be loved by My Father, and I will _Love_ him and _Manifest_ Myself to him."

The Lord promised to manifest Himself to us as we demonstrate love for Him. It is clear that we who love the Lord will do what He says. The reality of this is that God invites each of us to participate in His work on the earth. We are not called or commanded to simply know *about* God. Rather, we are invited into a true, loving relationship. This means we have opportunity to know what the Lord is doing and get involved. The result is true fulfillment.

If we want to know God's will, we must respond to His invitation to love and seek Him. We must not be satisfied to just know *about* God, when we can truly know

God by experience. This experience occurs as He reveals Himself to us through prayer, the Word, our worship, and even circumstances and people.

Moses learned about a relationship with God firsthand.

> *"Then Moses said to God, "Indeed, when I come to the children of Israel and say to them, 'The God of your fathers has sent me to you,' and they say to me, 'What is His name?' what shall I say to them?" {14} And God said to Moses, "I AM WHO I AM." And He said, "Thus you shall say to the children of Israel, 'I AM has sent me to you.'"*
> *Exodus 3:13-14*

God was saying to Moses, "I AM everything you need," and during the next forty years, Moses came to know God experientially as Jehovah or Yahweh, the Great I AM. God wants us to know Him by name just as Moses did. We come to know Him intimately as He reveals Himself to us through experience.

We become more intimately acquainted through personal worship. It is important for us to worship, bless, call upon, thank, trust, praise, and remember God by name.

The Lord takes initiative to pursue the relationship with us, so we must respond to His invitation through love. God is not interested in a one-sided love affair. He wants us to love and obey Him.

Points to remember:
- ◆ God is God; He never stops being God.
- ◆ God loves us; He never stops loving us.
- ◆ God knows and wants what is best for us.
- ◆ God is all-powerful and all-knowing.
- ◆ God is able to make us capable of doing His will.
- ◆ What God starts, He will finish.
- ◆ God speaks to us to accomplish His will.
- ◆ We must trust and obey (Hebrews 3:12,19; 4:11).
- ◆ Hebrews chapters 3 and 4 tell us that two sins kept the people of God from experiencing the fullness of His promises: lack of trust and disobedience.

If we really want to know what God is up to, we should talk to Him and ask questions, watch, listen, and look for ways to get involved in what He is doing.

Christ calls each of us to pursue a global purpose with a global vision. This is in direct opposition to worldly pursuits. When the Lord calls us, He does so with a purpose and mandate (commission). We, as disciples of the Lord Jesus Christ, are to become Great Commission Christians. This can only occur as we learn to listen.

God will speak. Will we hear?

> *"He who is of God hears God's words; therefore you do not hear, because you are not of God."*
> *John 8:47*

God's Spirit speaks through the Bible, prayer, circumstances, and the Church to reveal Himself, His purposes, and His ways. Throughout Scripture, we find that God spoke frequently to man. His methods varied from person to person; however, they knew it was God, and they knew what He said.

Although it is not wrong for us to look for open and closed doors or to ask God to stop us if we are in error, it is best to wait until we hear a clear word from God.

This often involves a process where we read the Word of134 God, the Bible. The Spirit reveals truth. We then adjust our life to the truth of God through obedient action. The Word then works in and through us to accomplish His purpose.

God also takes the initiative by causing us to want to pray. In the Spirit, we pray in agreement with the will of God and again must adjust our life to the truth of God. We can look and listen for confirmation or further direction from the Bible, circumstances, etc. As we obey, God works in and through us we experience Him on a daily basis.

This brings us to another crucial step in the process…

Faith That Works

Henry Blackaby refers to this next step in the process as *The Crisis Of Belief,* because very often, when God reveals what He wants to do through us, we face a *crisis*. In other words, we come to a point of decision. The Greek word is often translated *judgment*. It is much like reaching critical mass as in the world of science. Something must happen. This is actually a "turning point" in our lives as we must decide what we believe about God. How we respond at this turning point will determine whether we go on to be involved with God in something much greater than we are, or continue on our own way and miss what God has purposed for our lives. This is not a "one-time" experience, but a daily walk. How we live our lives is a testimony of what we think about God, how we see God, and what we believe about God. Biblical examples include Joshua preparing for battle upon entering the Land of Promise (Joshua 6:1-5), and Peter fetching a coin from the mouth of a fish (Matthew 17:24-27).

Do we ever sense that God wants to do something big, and as a result we face a crisis of belief? We should keep in mind that if God has asked us to do something, it is almost always bigger than we are. It is not possible for believers to accomplish what God calls us to do if God is not part of the equation. This is a fascinating truth: God does not call us to do what we can do without Him.

Faith is always required on our part; true faith requires action. It also demands a response to God's revelation (invitation) and exposes what we believe about God (our lives are a testimony).

Hebrews chapter 11 has been called the "Hall of Fame of Faith" because it includes a list of men and women who accomplished great things for the Lord.

As we read the chapter, we notice the break in time and events between verses 29 and 30:

> *"By faith they passed through the Red Sea as by dry land, whereas the Egyptians, attempting to do so, were drowned. {30} By faith the walls of Jericho fell down after they were encircled for seven days."*   *Hebrews 11:29-30*

Why is nothing recorded of the forty-year wilderness experience? The answer is simply that God requires His people to trust and obey, and this is where the Israelites fell painfully short.

What's Next?

So, now what must we do in order to fulfill God's will?

Read The Following Passage And Fill In The Blanks
LUKE 14:33

"So likewise, whoever of you does not _____ all that he

has _____ be My _____."

Something must happen at this point. For us to do what the Lord has spoken, we will have to make adjustments. Change is not always easy, but it is always needed in our lives as disciples, and *change is not change until it is change.*

Adjusting our lives to God is the next critical turning point in knowing and doing the will of God. We must believe that God is who He says He is and that He will do what He says He will do. Without faith in God, it is easy to make a mistake or wrong decision at the first turning point (crisis).

Making adjustments in our lives is equally important. If we choose to make the adjustment, we can go on to obedience. If we refuse to adjust, we risk missing God's best. The "crisis of belief" requires *faith.* Adjusting our lives requires *action.*

Once we come to a place of trusting God, we demonstrate faith by what we do. Obedience is part of the action required. Adjustments and obedience may be costly. When God speaks and reveals what He is doing, it is an invitation for us to adjust our lives and join Him. Once we make adjustments, we are in position to obey. It is very clear that we cannot remain as we are and go with God at the same time.

Consider the following:

- Noah could not continue life as usual and build the ark at the same time.
- Abram could not stay in Ur or Haran and father a nation in Canaan.
- Moses could not stay on the backside of the desert.
- David had to leave the sheep to become king.
- Peter, James, and John had to leave their fishing business to follow Jesus.
- Matthew had to leave his tax collector booth to follow Christ.
- Saul of Tarsus (Paul) had to change his direction in order to be used by God.

Once adjustments are made, God begins to move. This may be the single greatest difficulty in following Christ. We tend to want to skip this reality and just move on to obedience.

Luke 18:18-27 tells a story about a rich, young ruler who was not willing to make the adjustment and follow Christ. In the end, he missed out on great blessing. Adjustments are not always easy, and may, in fact, be difficult and challenging.

Changes in circumstances, relationships, thinking, commitments, actions, and even beliefs are often involved. These adjustments come at the point of taking action by faith. The easier part of the equation is experienced when we face the crisis of belief and must decide what we believe about God. The more difficult part is adjusting our lives and taking action that demonstrates faith. We may have to attempt things that only God can do, where before we only did what we knew we could do. Obedience may be costly as it might involve a change in our programs or agendas. It may also include enduring opposition and require depending totally on God to work through us and around us.

Obedience Is Better Than Sacrifice

To experience God at work in and through us, we must obey Him. When we obey Him, He will accomplish His work through us. Thus, we will know Him by experience. When God gives a directive, we are to obey. Obedience is the outward expression of our love for God.

Read The Following Passage And Fill In The Blanks
JOHN 14:23

"Jesus answered and said to him, "If anyone _____*love*_____ Me,

he will _____*Keep*_____ My word; and My Father will

_____*Love*_____ him, and We will come to him and make

Our _____*OBODE*_____ with him.""

King Saul is a good example of a man who failed to obey God yet wanted to appease Him with a sacrifice (1 Samuel 15:15). Perhaps Saul thought he could act in such a manner because he was king. What he failed to understand is that there are spiritual boundaries in God's kingdom, and when people refuse to submit themselves and honor those boundaries, they are subject to fail. King Saul did not adjust his life and act with faith according to the command he was given. As a result, he lost his authority.

Faith that does not follow through with action is dead (James 2:17, 20). Obedience brings joy and uninterrupted fellowship with God. The Lord is interested in developing our character and will not give up on us, even when we fall, as long as we are humble and submit to His authority. We must begin by doing what we already know to do. Disobedience can be very costly. Affirmation comes after obedience.

God reveals Himself through what He does and will never give us an assignment for which He has not equipped us. God, who initiates His work with us, is the One who guarantees to complete it.

> *"Being confident of this very thing, that He who has begun a good work in you will complete it until the day of Jesus Christ."*   *Philippians 1:6*

We must allow God as much time as needed to complete the work. Whatever God has for us to do must be important in His eyes. We need to keep in mind that God has called us into a relationship with Him. It is unwise for us to take things into our own hands. It is vital that we know God well enough that if something does not measure up to His ways, we will recognize it and turn away. The Lord enables us to accomplish the tasks He assigns for our lives; we must believe and begin to act according to His instructions.

It may be necessary for us to review these seven points from *Experiencing God* once again. We should take time to seek the Lord and learn to hear His voice. God is inviting each of us to participate in His great plan; not His plan for us, but for the world.

As Christ's disciples, we must take a good look at our lives and make adjustments. In other words, reorder our lives where necessary. Is Christ the center? Is His will more important than our own? Are we willing to take time to seek God in order to find Him?

Read The Following Passage And Fill In The Blanks
JEREMIAH 33:3

" _____Come_____ to Me, and I will _____

you, and _____ you great and mighty things, which you do not

_____."

Here is how the Amplified Bible states Jeremiah 33:3, "Call to Me and I will answer you and show you great and mighty things, fenced in and hidden, which you do not know (do not distinguish and recognize, have knowledge of and understand)."

There are many things God wants to reveal that have been hidden. This includes things that have been fenced in, things we cannot know until the Lord reveals them. The key to revelation is our seeking. If we are genuine in our desire and quest in regard to having knowledge of God's will and ways, He will surely be faithful to bring understanding.

The problem is often seen in what we seek or pursue. Furthermore, we must begin to see things from a biblical perspective and stop making excuses.

It may be true, at least in the area of psychology, that we are a product of our education, environment, and experience; however, God can use all of those things to bring us to where He wants us to be.

We must avoid seeing things as the world sees them. This may include our own lives. After all, Sarah saw herself as too old to have children and laughed at the prospect when the Word came forth (so did Abraham). God proved Himself faithful with the birth of Isaac. Prophet Jeremiah evidently considered himself too young to be used of God. The Lord proved the man wrong and even rebuked him.

"Then said I: "Ah, Lord GOD! Behold, I cannot speak, for I am a youth." {7} But the LORD said to me: "Do not say, 'I am a youth,' For you shall go to all to whom I send you, And whatever I command you, you shall speak. {8} Do not be afraid of their faces, For I am with you to deliver you," says the LORD."

Jeremiah 1:6-8

The Bible records that Jeremiah was one of the great prophets who spoke forth God's oracles of truth. Any of us can think of reasons that God cannot or should not use us. Keep in mind that He has already chosen us as His elect. Believers must cast down every thought that is contrary to God's will and Word in order to become all that He has called us to be and accomplish what He has ordained us to do.

Moses was eighty years old when he finally recognized God's plan unfolding. He had fled the comfortable lifestyle in Egypt and spent approximately forty years in Midian. Moses may have considered if the things that were in his heart as a young man would ever take place. God had a plan and purpose for Moses, and it really began to unfold and develop when he was much older. Perhaps there were things that God had to deal with in His perfect time and fashion.

The same is true in our lives today. Just as the Lord called Moses and revealed His will, He has a plan for each of us. God will reveal His purpose through His Spirit and Word. We must simply remain pliable in the hands of the Master and allow Him to complete His perfect work in and through our lives.

It would benefit us to keep Philippians 2:13 in mind: "for it is God who works in you both to will and to do for His good pleasure."

God will be faithful to complete the work He has begun. We must have confidence in His ability to finish what He has started. God has chosen us and desires to fashion us for His pleasure. As a new creation in Christ, we can have confidence that the past does not have to dictate our future! Our future really does look brighter than the past.

As we walk with God daily, His thoughts can be our thoughts. Our ways can be His ways as we are conformed into the man or woman that He wants us to be. This really is not a hard or difficult thing. It simply takes time and a willing heart. Attitudes may need to be adjusted to receive all God has for His people.

Our minds can be renewed if we believe we have received the mind of Christ as a result of the new birth (1 Corinthians 2:16). It is our responsibility to present our lives to God as a sacrifice that is acceptable, in order to demonstrate His good and perfect will (Romans 12:1-2). However, it is difficult and challenging to be conformed to the world and transformed in our thinking at the same time. Therefore, we must give ourselves continually to the Word of God. Paul, the apostle, spoke of his own life when addressing the Philippian believers. He wrote, "I press on, that I may lay hold of that for which Christ Jesus has also laid hold of me" (Philippians 3:12). Paul was running after a prize that was set in front of him.

Read The Following Passage And Fill In The Blanks
PHILIPPIANS 3:13-14

"Brethren, I do not count myself to have apprehended; but ___*one*___

thing I do, ___*forgetting*___ those things which are

behind and ___*reaching*___ forward to those

things which are ahead, {14} I ___*press*___ toward the

goal for the prize of the upward call of God in Christ Jesus."

The apostle reveals some very important truths. It is vital that we learn to let go of things in the past. This does not mean that we forget; it does mean that we choose to *let go*. It is not possible to hold on to the past and *reach* for what lies ahead. We can never hope to get a hold on something when our hands are full. We need to let go of yesterday, because it simply is not as important as today and tomorrow. There is a prize or goal that is set before each of us. The "upward call of God" cannot be fulfilled in and of ourselves. We need the Lord and one another in order to accomplish our purpose in life.

We must see ourselves as part of something much bigger. We need Christ at the center of our lives, and we need each other to fulfill the divine plan. God does not want to use some of us; He wants to use all of us to reach the world and touch others with His love and grace.

Genesis 12 show how Abram did as God told him. Abram had no one to teach him. He recognize the voice of the Lord

Mat 6. Seek 1st the kingdom of God & His righteousness

Love, trust & obey Him

LESSON SUMMARY

THE GREATEST PRIVILEGE WE HAVE AS BELIEVERS IN JESUS CHRIST IS TO experience God in a real and personal way. It is a marvelous realization of truth that the Lord, Creator of heaven and earth, desires to reveal Himself and His will to us. Too often, we take for granted the relationship God offers, and we do not fully experience all He's made available. We may believe that God is at work around us, but to walk in a day-to-day relationship with Him, knowing that He has invited us to be involved in His work on the earth, is perhaps difficult to comprehend. This entire experience requires faith and obedience. As we learn to trust, it becomes easier to obey and make the adjustments or changes necessary to see the fullness of God's will perfected. It was the lack of faith and obedience that kept the children of Israel from the Land of Promise. The same is true for us today. If we refuse to believe and walk in accordance with God's will, we too, may spend years wandering in the wilderness. We could die and never experience the fullness of God's purpose. There is something God wants us to begin doing today. We must be willing to wait on Him to reveal His plan to us. He does this step-by-step, not all at once, for that would likely be overwhelming. There is no greater reward, no greater fulfillment in life, than that which comes from knowing and doing the will of God who made us. This is the meaning of true success in life: knowing and doing the will of the One who created us. God does His part, we must simply trust and obey Him on a daily basis. We should be encouraged. We may start today, and spend time experiencing the Lord in a very real and relevant way. It will change our lives forever!

"But as it is written: "Eye has not seen, nor ear heard, Nor have entered into the heart of man The things which God has prepared for those who love Him."
1 Corinthians 2:9

QUESTIONS
for REVIEW

1. Could it be possible that God in heaven, the Creator of all things, really wants to speak to us individually?

   _____

2. What are the three facets of relationship that Paul describes in 2 Corinthians 13:14?

   _____

   _____

   _____

3. As found in this lesson, there are several things we can do in preparation for hearing God. What are they?

   _____

   _____

   _____

4. Are there times when you will hear the Spirit of the Lord say something to your heart that is contrary to the Bible?

   _____

   _____

5. We are clearly told in Matthew 6:33-34 what we are to pursue first. Write the answer:

   _____

   _____

6. We will face only one crisis of belief in our spiritual walk.

   True   ~~False~~

7. One of the ways we experience God is through obedience.

   ~~True~~   False

8. Faith that does not follow through with action is dead.

   ~~True~~   False

9. Write out the seven spiritual realities to hearing and experiencing God.

   _____

   _____

   _____

   _____

   _____

   _____

   _____

IN CONCLUSION, THE PURPOSE OF THIS COURSE IS TO ASSIST THE YOUNG BELIEVER'S growth in their walk with Christ. We trust that goal has been achieved. We began by discussing the need for change in various areas of life: social, sexual, and church. From that beginning point to this final page, we have walked through a process involving the various baptisms relevant to the believer. Hopefully, the Bible has become more alive as we have learned to accurately understand, through the proper study of its contents, what it is communicating.

The material also covered teaching about Jesus Christ in respect to what He has done and what He continues to do on our behalf. In addition, we should now have a firm grasp on our need to pray, fast, and journal as we experience God on a daily basis.

He really is at work all around us, and He has invited us to join in His work here on the earth. This does lead us to a *crisis of belief,* as the Lord is stretching us spiritually, mentally, and perhaps emotionally.

We encourage you to take the next step in your own discipleship process as Level One is just "the tip of the iceberg," and there is so much more to learn and do in order to grow strong and fruitful for the Lord.

Experience has taught us that being involved with a small group of dedicated Christians is absolutely the best way to grow. Therefore, we encourage you to get connected if you have not already done so. In addition, continue seeking God by taking the next step in Ministry Training School, Level Two, where we will persist in making solid progress as disciples and begin to produce much fruit for the glory of our Father in heaven.

God has called us to bear fruit and glorify His name in all the earth. In order to accomplish this, we must be properly trained.

It is our hope and prayer that this course has been a help in achieving that goal, and it is also our prayer that each student of the Word will move on to the next level and fulfill the high calling of God in Christ Jesus.

"Brethren, I do not count myself to have apprehended; but one thing I do, forgetting those things which are behind and reaching forward to those things which are ahead, {14} I press toward the goal for the prize of the upward call of God in Christ Jesus."
Philippians 3:13-14

Lesson One

Scripture Fill-Ins

Page 10 ....Christ, Creation, Passed, All

Page 11 .... Whoever, Deny, Cross, Follow

Page 12 ....Chosen, Royal, Holy, Special, Darkness, Light

Page 13 ....Sanctify, Hearts, Ready, Reason, Meekness

Page 15 .... Stones, House, Priesthood, Sacrifices

Page 16 ....Honorable, Undefiled, Fornicators, Adulterers

Page 17 .... Lord, Good, Alone, Helper

Page 18 ....Sexual, Sin, Immorality, Body, Temple, God

Page 19 .... Tempted, Desires, Sin, Death

Page 20 ....Instruments, Alive, Righteousness, Dominion

Page 21 ....Redemption, Forgiveness, Grace

Page 24 .... Consider, Love, Exhorting

Questions For Review

1. 2 Corinthians 5:17 .... Page 10

2. 1 Peter 2:9 .... Page 12

3. Any three: Friends (Relationships), Habits, Thought Patterns,
    Behavior .... Page 12

4. Genesis 2:18 .... Page 17

5. True .... Page 17

6. True .... Page 18

7. True .... Page 18

8. Look, Lust, Linger .... Page 19

9. True .... Page 20

10. True .... Page 22

11. True .... Page 22

12. d. All of the above .... Page 24

Lesson Two

Scripture Fill-Ins

Page 31 .... Body, Spirit, Lord, Faith, Baptism

Page 32 .... Born Again, See

Page 34 .... Go, Disciples, Baptizing

Page 35 .... Baptized, Water, Son, Pleased

Page 38 .... Heart, Spirit, Heart, Spirit

Page 39 .... One, Suddenly, Fire, Filled, Tongues

Page 40 .... Signs, Believe

Page 42 .... Thirsts, Drink, Believes, Heart, Spirit, Receive

Questions For Review

1. Seven .... Page 29

2. Christ's Body, Water, Holy Spirit .... Page 30

3. True .... Page 30

4. Baptisma: to fully immerse, to dip under and up; to bury
   into regardless of the element used .... Page 30

5. To follow Christ's example. It is a command found in the Word
   of God. .... Pages 33-34

6. Jordan River .... Page 33

7. False .... Page 34

8. False .... Page 36

9. True .... Page 39

10. True .... Page 41

11. The Holy Spirit .... Page 42

Lesson Three

Scripture Fill-Ins

Questions For Review

Lesson Four

Scripture Fill-Ins

Page 75 .... Alienated, Wicked, Reconciled, Death, Blameless
Page 76 .... Griefs, Sorrows, Wounded, Bruised, Peace, Healed, Astray, Iniquity
Page 77 .... Jesus, Veil, Two, Earth, Rocks
Page 78 .... Heart, Spirit, Stone, Flesh, My, My, My
Page 80 .... Dead, Alive, All, Wiped, Nailed, Powers, Triumphing
Page 81 .... Adversary, Devour, Resist
Page 82 .... Kings, Priests, Reign
Page 84 .... Loved, Gave, Believes, Perish, Life, Condemn, Saved
Page 85 .... Thief, Steal, Kill, Destroy, Life, Abundantly
Page 86 .... All, Christ, Strengthens
Page 88 .... Jesus, Authority, Go, Disciples, Baptizing
Page 89 .... Confidence, Him, Anything, Will, Know, Know, Asked
Page 90 .... Agree, Anything, Ask, Gathered, Name
Page 91 .... Disarmed, Triumphing
Page 94 .... Law, Purified, Blood, Remission
Page 95 .... Mediator, New, Blood, Speaks, Abel
Page 96 .... Justified, Peace
Page 97 .... Body, You, Bought, God's
Page 98 .... Light, Fellowship, Blood, All

Questions For Review

1. It was due to the fact that through His death, burial, and
   resurrection, sinful man could once again be
   reconciled to a holy God .... Page 75

2. Fulfill it .... Page 75

3. Yes .... Page 76

4. c. Veil .... Page 77

5. True .... Page 85

6. Power to be righteous, Actual adoption or "sonship,"
   Freedom from sin, Love for the brethren, Love for God,
   Power to keep God's commandments, Power to overcome
   the world, Freedom from Satan .... Page 82

7. d. All of the above .... Page 85

8. True .... Page 87

9. False .... Page 93

10. False .... Page 98

Lesson Five

Scripture Fill-Ins

Questions For Review

Lesson Six

Scripture Fill-Ins

Questions For Review

1. Blackaby, Henry T., and King, Claude V., *Experiencing God*, Nashville, Tennessee, LifeWay Press, 1990

2. Gesenius, William, *A Hebrew and English Lexicon*, Oxford, Claredon Press, 1974

3. Strong, James, *Strong's Exhaustive Concordance*, New Jersey, Madison, 1890

4. Thayer, Joseph Henry, D. D., *Thayer's Greek-English Lexicon*, Grand Rapids, Michigan, Associated Publishers & Authors Inc., 1885

5. Thorndike, E. L., and Barnhart, Clarence L., *Scott, Foresman Advanced Dictionary*, Glenview, Illinois, 1983

6. Vine, W.E., *An Expository Dictionary of New Testament Words*, Old Tappan, New Jersey, Fleming H. Revell Company, 1966

7. Merriam-Webster, *Merriam-Webster's Collegiate Dictionary*, Tenth Edition, Springfield, Massachusetts, 1993

8. Great Site Website